Reflections on Grace

Reflections on Grace

Thomas A. Langford

Foreword by
William H. Willimon

Edited and introduced by
Philip A. Rolnick & Jonathan R. Wilson

Cascade Books
A division of *Wipf & Stock Publishers*
199 West 8th Avenue, Suite 3 • Eugene OR 97401

REFLECTIONS ON GRACE

Copyright © 2007 Ann Marie Langford. All rights reserved. Except for brief quotations in critical publications or reviews, no part of this book may be reproduced in any manner without prior written permission from the publisher. Write: Permissions, Wipf & Stock, 199 W. 8th Ave., Eugene, OR 97401.

ISBN 13: 978-1-55635-058-0

Cataloging-in-Publication data:

Reflections on grace / Thomas A. Langford.

xii + 114 p.; 23 cm.

ISBN 13: 978-1-55635-058-0

1. Grace (Theology). I. Title

BT761 .L35 2007

Manufactured in the U.S.A.

Contents

Foreword
Saying Grace: Tom Langford vii
by William H. Willimon

Acknowledgements xi

Introduction
A Work of Grace, a Life of Grace 1
by Philip A. Rolnick & Jonathan R. Wilson

1 : Grace as Giver 17

2 : Grace and Truth 33

3 : Grace and the Biblical Jesus 49

4 : Grace and Creation 63

5 : Grace upon Grace 81

6 : Grace, Disgrace, Grace 99

Bibliography 111

FOREWORD

Saying Grace: Tom Langford

He was gracious, grateful, full of grace. Who better to teach us grace than one who so genially embodied, personified, and incarnated grace? You will find in the pages of this book that Tom Langord's particular grace is not the rip-roaring, frontier Methodist revival, conversionist, and disruptive sort of grace. Commenting upon his faith, Langford mused, "With Horace Bushnell, I can say that I never knew a time when I was not a Christian." Blessed by a serenity of spirit, he felt no need to venture far beyond his native North Carolina, or his school, Duke University. He never wandered from his Methodist upbringing, knew neither a dark night of the soul nor tortured battles with God. He had this easy, quietly confident (gracious?) relationship with God that did not waver, despite his thorough immersion in the best and deepest of classical and contemporary philosophy. Perhaps he always knew that our relationship with God is essentially the result, not of our thoughtful effort or anxious striving, but due to grace, God's grace.

Langford said that he hoped his "narrow limitation of geographical existence" did not imply "a narrowly limited vision or a lack of . . . human sympathy which is any less inclusive than the world." He called his own history "not strikingly unusual," so I won't linger long upon it here, except to say that it formed him into a wonderfully unhurried, not-too-driven personality with a brilliant, but never obvious or ostentatious mind. I once commented to him on his serenity, and he attributed that to the early death of his father. Bereavement had taught him that life was a brief, fragile gift. It seemed typical of Tom Langford to turn even that boyhood sadness into grace.

He was a son of the church and credited the church with embracing him with a succession of loving, wise father-figures who guided him. These church members, along with his strong mother, instilled in him that he had been given great gifts by God and that those gifts were also a gracious assignment to serve God.

In college, while he was a student preacher serving a little Methodist church, he fell in love with philosophy, or as he said it, with persons who loved philosophy. Looking back on that awakening, Tom Langford said that true intellectual development is always dependent upon a student's transforming encounter with "a challenging person with provocative ideas." That was the teacher he became at Duke. Although he had little use for the "Personalism" that captured early twentieth-century philosophy among many Methodists, he always practiced a person-centered, personable mode of philosophizing. I remember complaining to him about the lack of progress we were making on the Curriculum Committee at the Divinity School. Dean Langford (who had appointed me to the Curriculum Committee) surprised me by saying, "I find it difficult to work up much interest in tinkering with the curriculum. Change the curriculum all you want and you're still stuck with the same people who will probably teach as they have always taught. A university isn't about curriculum; it's about people in conversation with other people."

"Have you ever read Proust?" I asked him one day, telling Langford of my newfound enthusiasm for the master of French introspection.

He replied, "I tire of Proust's relish of decadence and his subjectivity. I'm more interested in novelists who are more interested in other people than in themselves."

Earlier, when asked to write about the early stages of his intellectual journey, Langford said that throughout his growth as a young scholar, he had been able to maintain a "vivid sense of God." When he came to seminary at Duke in 1951, he searched philosophy and Wesleyan theology for "the most adequate way of interpreting . . . spiritual experience." (A fairly typical Methodist experiential-expressivist, liberal, mid-twentieth-century way of talking about the Christian faith.) Yet at seminary "a Christological interpretation of my experience returned as the most adequate mode of explanation."

As you read Langford's explication of grace, I believe that you will witness his continued growth in grace. What could have been (and in places in this book is) a rather detached, somewhat abstract treatise on grace, is from the first a specifically Christological mediation. If the book seems uneven or undeveloped in places, it's because it is a work in progress, as was Tom Langford's whole journey with Jesus. You are witnessing his continued growth in grace, even late in his career, as a philosophical theologian. It is as if here, at the end of his life, he is retrieving his earlier youthful awareness that grace has a name, a face, a definite contour and specific attributes—Jesus Christ. Here the one who began his work as a philosophical theologian, a sort of Methodist Tillichian, returns home to testify to that which philosophy cannot teach. He becomes not the philosophical explicator but a witness to the grace that has met him throughout his life in Christ. We have here the fruit of one whose devotional life was disciplined and well practiced, one who with his beloved Ann Marie delighted in the intricacies of the gift of friendship with God in Christ.

When asked, mid-career, about the goal of his teaching in the university, Tom said that his purpose was to teach in such a way that he brought "a word of grace to the world and critical self-appraisal to the church," a bold and rare statement for a professor in a university Department of Religion. It's almost unimaginable today, in a university world where academic administrators are now rarely intellectuals and almost never publicly confessing Christians, that someone of Langford's scholarly stature and unashamed faith commitment was for so long a term so widely admired as a Provost of Duke University.

I recall the Duke Trustee who told me with tears in his eyes about the debate that had just occurred in the Board concerning divestment of the University from corporations that do business with apartheid South Africa. He said that the debate was following the dictates of commonsense business and that things were not moving toward divestment until Provost Langford asked for the floor. Langford spoke to the Board for but a few minutes about the moral purpose of the university, the need for the university to teach the students not only how to think but how to live by its own ethical action, telling them that Duke was not just another university, but one founded by the Methodists for a reason. The vote was taken immediately and was overwhelming for divestment.

"I've never been more proud of this university," said the Trustee, "Tom reminded us of what God expected."

Upon his seventieth birthday in February of 1999, grateful students presented Langford with a Festschrift, aptly titled, *Grace Upon Grace: Essays in Honor of Thomas A. Langford.* He taught Christian grace in the manner of the great classical philosophers whom he so admired by embodying in his life that which he professed in his books, in the classroom, and in the pulpit. How appropriate that this manuscript was lying upon his desk when he died. What grace that we have it now. Grace, pure grace.

A woman who served for years as Tom Langford's administrative assistant said of him at his death, "If he ever erred, he always erred on the side of grace."

William H. Willimon
Bishop, the Birmingham, Alabama
Area of the United Methodist Church

Acknowledgements

The editors would like to thank Ann Marie Langford for sending us so many of her husband's unpublished papers and other documents that greatly assisted us in our work. We also are indebted to Jeremy Kidwell for his work on the endnote references. Likewise, we would like to thank Laura Stierman and Laurie Dimond, who, by electronically scanning the original manuscript, were able to get the manuscript into a form that we could then edit. We would also like to thank Jeremy Funk, the copyeditor at Wipf and Stock, for his careful reading and queries. Finally, we would like to thank Charlie Collier, the extraordinary Acquisitions Editor at Wipf and Stock, who once took a graduate course from Tom Langford and whose ideas for this project have been very helpful.

INTRODUCTION

A Work of Grace, A Life of Grace

Philip A. Rolnick and Jonathan R. Wilson

Reflections on Grace is not a complete systematic theology of grace, but it is the legacy of a complete life that was filled with grace. Thomas A. Langford (1929–2000) grew up in Charlotte, North Carolina, and graduated from nearby Davidson College. In 1951 he married Ann Marie Daniel. Their forty-eight years together saw the birth of four sons and numerous grandchildren, and their home become a hospitable center for extended family, friends, and visitors from around the world. Langford was very much a son of the South, but he was a Southerner whose interest and influence was worldwide. When visiting the Langford home, one might easily come upon guests from Singapore, the Czech Republic, Austria, England, and any and all other points of the globe. His global contacts and friendships were in many ways the fruit of his belief in the boundlessness of God's grace.

In 1952 Tom Langford was ordained a Methodist minister, and in 1958 he received his doctorate from Duke University. Throughout his adult life Langford served both church and academy. His personal formation in the church and his ongoing devotion to it shaped his performance in the academy, and his scholarship, broad experience with diverse students, faculty, and administrators, likewise bolstered what he could bring to the church.

In his academic career at Duke, Langford was a Professor in the Department of Religion from 1956–65, Chair of the Department from 1965–71, Dean of the Duke Divinity School from 1971–81, a Divinity School Professor from 1981–84, Vice Provost of the University from 1984–88, the inaugural William Kellon Quick Professor of

Theology and Methodist Studies from 1986–97, and Provost of the University from 1990–94. He published some fourteen books and over sixty articles and essays, and he was given a host of the most prestigious academic awards. In this distinguished 41-year academic career, it would be hard to overestimate the influence that Langford had on undergraduate and graduate students, seminary students, colleagues, administrators, and even North Carolina political figures. At the time of his death, then Duke President Nannerl Keohane wrote that he was "a wonderful colleague, advisor and friend. He was truly one of the wisest and most thoughtful people I've ever known . . . [a] most amazing mentor, advisor and guide. I relied enormously on his judgment . . . I was very fortunate that he was in the provost's office when I got to Duke. At that point, he was my closest colleague." Over the years so many people came to Langford for counsel when facing tough situations that he gained a reputation that is accurately attested in Keohane's tribute.

There was never anything pretentious about Langford. He ably wielded positions of responsibility because he knew that his primary responsibility was to God. His life and his *reflections on grace* are of one piece. Langford always had something to give to others who came to him because he knew himself to be a son of divine grace. He had an uncanny ability to focus on the person with whom he was meeting. He did so not as some sort of technique, but rather, because he understood the gospel to be about a relationship to God that always played out as a relationship to people. When required to write a short faculty autobiography during his first years at Duke (something he rather disliked doing), Langford reflected:

> My educational experience seems, in reflection, also to hinge upon persons. My development was enhanced by interaction with others. Perhaps the awareness and conviction that life is found only in encounter, in meeting with others, has been in large measure the contribution of my past; in any case, it does play a decisive role in my theological constructions as well as in my existential commitment to the present—for the present

is presence—and the high valuation which I place upon the devotional life and human relationships.[1]

Many of the central themes of *Reflections on Grace*, e.g., the emphasis on *persons*, on encounter, on the "commitment to the present," are foreshadowed in this early statement.

Langford's academic career was paralleled by his church career. In addition to having served several churches as a young man, countless appearances as guest preacher, retreat leader, and Sunday school teacher, he served in a variety of denominational tasks from 1972 until he died. In 1988 he was the primary author of the revision of the United Methodist Church's "Our Theological Task"; with his wife Ann Marie he wrote various inspirational books for lay people; and in 1999 he presented a paper on grace to the United Methodist Council of Bishops.

Earlier, in 1992, he had become Chair of the Rural Church Division. In this capacity he served churches throughout North and South Carolina. For some, serving rural churches might not be the fulfillment of their career desires, but for Langford it was a privilege and a joy. In a private conversation he once told of a divinity student who had been sent as an intern to a rural North Carolina community. Upon his return Langford asked the young man about his experience there. When the intern complained about having wasted his time where there was a lack of activity and culture, Langford strongly rebuked him for having squandered a unique opportunity to learn something about farming, farm community, and especially, *farmers*. He even told him that he should probably not become a minister unless he learned to appreciate the unique problems, concerns, and gifts that people actually have.

For Langford, the gospel was not an abstract concept; it was a relationship with God that fostered relationship and community with people. Although Langford was an irenic man, he was also decisive and determined. He believed that the pervasiveness of human sin required what he called "strong grace," yet another theme of *Reflections on Grace*. This kind of strong grace could encounter others, touch them

---

1. Langford, "Focus on Faculty."

"without bruising" (see chapter 1) and thereby invite them into the communal relationship of grace.

Langford's deepest theological convictions manifested in his personal relations precisely because he thought that those personal relations were the practical realization of the gospel. Langford was equally happy advising United States senators (he was a close friend and advisor of Terry Sanford) or spending a Sunday afternoon eating and conversing with folks from a rural parish. To him all were capable of realizing a divine destiny and noble identity. His interest, in both church and academy, was to call people into that identity or to foster it in those already possessed of it. As he puts it:

> A generous person is of noble lineage, high born—this used to apply to human status, nobility. But who is of the noblest lineage, the highest born? Is it not those who are sons and daughters of God? It is from this heritage that we are given our status, our character.
>
> The generosity of God evokes our generosity; like parent, like child. "Love one another as I have loved you." (John 13:34)[2]

Langford's bipartite career in the Methodist Church and at Duke University were unified in his balanced approach to the problems of the twentieth century, problems that affected both church and academy. In a Founder's Day sermon preached at the Duke Chapel in 1985, Langford observed that, forty years previously, the Chapel symbolized something of a common consensus, but with the increasing dominance of Enlightenment thinking, consensus around the Chapel was no longer present. Without utterly discounting Enlightenment thinking, he warned:

> Indeed, one can say that the Enlightenment, with its drive to remove limiting dogmatisms and unacceptable restrictions, has tended at times imperialistically to impose its own dogmatisms and restrictions.
>
> One always has to be careful. The iconoclasts, those who destroy idols, are often themselves idolaters.[3]

---

2. Taken from Langford's unpublished "Notebooks of Prayers."
3. Langford, "Religion and Sound Learning," slightly altered.

Being careful, taking into account as much relevant information as possible, was a Langford trademark, as was his abiding suspicion of alleged truths which only ended up reducing or narrowing human life. Resisting hegemonic secularization, he proposed a post-consensus role for the Chapel and all that it symbolizes, a role of "dialogical partnership" in which Christian faith would remain part of a conversation of "mutual challenge, mutual respect, but also mutual argumentation."[4] Langford recognized that intellectual integrity and faith needed one another. Without the other, the intellect "can be put to the use of terrible masters," and faith "can quickly become self-serving and represent the most oppressive forms of pride."[5]

"Conversation" was one of Langford's favorite metaphors—not surprising for one whose life was a sort of conversation between the academic and ecclesial. In an address to the Council of Methodist bishops, he delves into the roots of the term:

> Changes in the English language are at times instructive. Elizabethan English used the word "conversation" to mean life. For instance, in the King James Version of Philippians 1:27, "only let your conversation be as becometh the gospel of Christ . . ." This used to mean, as the Revised Standard Version translates it, "manner of life." Or in Hebrews 13:5, "let your conversation be without covetousness . . ." the Revised Standard Version reads, "keep your life without . . ." Again, the reference is to behavior, to the way one lives. In a profound sense, the Elizabethans were correct: life is conversation; it is interaction with God, with our sisters and brothers in Christ, with our neighbors.[6]

As a true conversationalist, Langford was loved and respected not only in the church that he served throughout his life, but also by those who had never darkened the door of a church. He was well aware of his twofold mission:

> I teach theology to the university students and philosophy of religion to the Divinity School students. This bringing of

---

4. Ibid.
5. Ibid.
6. Langford, "Distinctively Methodist."

the word of grace to the world and critical self-appraisal to the church constitute the two foci of my teaching and of my life."[7]

Langford was a balanced man who had a knack for contributing whatever was missing to achieve balance in a situation or institution.

As Langford took on ever weightier responsibility over the course of his life, he would return to this manuscript from time to time, hoping to develop it into a major work as "A Theology of Grace." As it turned out, his responsibilities at Duke and his health did not allow him the time and energy to complete the work. In a conversation about eight years before he died, he acknowledged that he was content not to complete this work, that he had come to recognize that his calling for the rest of his life was elsewhere. When asked if we (his former students) might continue his work on this project, he replied that it was up to us to make that judgment. Because the six chapters that he more or less completed contain so many gems, we decided to make the work available. Our hope is that ministers and lay people will find ample material here for sermons and church class topics and that readers of all sorts will find fresh ways to think about grace. In this manuscript, Langford has not systematically addressed every significant question about grace, but he has provided remarkable insights.

The text of *Reflections on Grace* has undergone our editorial revisions, but all of its ideas are Langford's. For the most part, we simply removed repetitions and rearranged some materials for greater clarity. In one or two cases we have removed several pages where Langford had begun some rather complex themes without sufficient clarification to be helpfully included.

Because "grace" brings to mind many different and even conflicting images, Langford's *Reflections on Grace* will serve to affirm and correct, to clarify and demarcate. Langford's grace was far more than a religious scheme of niceness and cordiality. He certainly possessed the "social graces," but he conceived grace as something far greater than mere cordiality and avoidance of conflict in a conspiracy of niceness. He knew quite profoundly that the human predicament required a

---

7. Langford, "Focus on Faculty."

radical remaking of our lives and our world, and he believed that the redemptive power of grace could meet this predicament. If grace is redemption, not merely improvement, the condition that it comes to must be in need of radical change.

In Langford's understanding, grace is more than God's work. When grace is working in our lives, we are not only engaged with the benefits of God, we are engaged with God. Although we may distinguish between the person and works of God, we may not separate them. God's work of grace is not only for us, it is the hospitable gift of relationship with us. The work of redemption is complete—indeed, it is redemptive—only when it brings us into right relationship with God—and then with one another. Grace is God's gift of Godself that transforms by the very activity of relationship. But where work connotes exertion, task, and duty, the graced relationship with God is characterized by delight.

As we saw foreshadowed above in the young Langford's "existential commitment to the present," his more mature theology is an unremitting focus on what he calls "God present" (see chapter 1 and passim). In chapter 6 he argues that, for theology, presence is not a problem but a presupposition. Presence is not to be found at the conclusion of a debate but at the commencement of life in Christ. Cultivating this divine presence in Christ, we can think, feel, and act under the aegis of "strong grace." All that we do and all that we are is formed out of this relationship with one who is not absent. For Langford, grace is not merely something that God gives. Rather, grace is a person; grace is Jesus Christ.

In Langford's thought Christ opens creation up to the full range of its possibilities. He thus advocated both *creatio ex nihilo*, the original divine act of creation out of nothing, as well as *creatio continua*, the notion that God present actively continues to foster the creativity of creation. Undoubtedly, this conviction encouraged him to pursue the creative possibilities of engaging academic life.

Langford contended that truth is alignment with God present. He thus writes of the "truing" of human life. Through Christ, creation, which had been misaligned, is reordered. Thus, doctrines are not ends in themselves but are guidelines that help us to know how to tell the story of God's grace rightly and to live with gracious integrity. Hence, truth is more than cognitive; it is mind, heart, and hands learning to be conformed to Christ. Truth, like everything else of importance for Langford, stems from and must be spoken from the relationship to God. In this relational understanding, we are servants of truth, never its master.

The realization of truth (and all other things noble in human experience) begins with the relationship that God has initiated on our behalf—with grace; hence, Langford personally placed a great value upon humility and considered humility a requirement of Christian self-awareness. But he was not one of those people who are proud of being humble. He so strongly disparaged focus on the self and its achievements because he knew that great achievement was far more likely by focusing on God. Langford once told a group of Methodist ministers that "we progress far more spiritually by spending five minutes looking at Christ than taking thirty minutes looking at ourselves."[8]

Likewise, becoming a Christian is no reason for pride, for the significance of Christianity is not in Christianity; it is in the God to whom Christianity refers. Langford thus would have Christianity itself be humbled by the astounding gift that it has been given. Speaking on another occasion to a gathering of Methodist bishops he said: "We are both in orders and under orders."[9]

Given his stress on humility, he felt that Christians and Christianity should be open to dialogue with non-Christian religions, for God's presence should be honored wherever it is expressed (see chapter 5). Langford wanted to eschew all comparisons of relative worth between Christianity and other religions. To him, humbling ourselves before the one we confess as Lord was of utmost significance so that we could begin to share with others the grace that we had already received.

Langford's unfailing relational focus of grace subtly transforms the "Boston personalism" that dominated academic Methodist theology in the middle of the twentieth century. That school of personalism was also known as "personal idealism." Where Boston personalism

---

8. An address given at Greensboro College, October 8, 1996.
9. "Distinctively Methodist."

moved too quickly into the theoretical and abstract, Langford retains a steady focus on the practical, cultural, and relational.

While Langford knew German theology well, he seemed to prefer the grace of personal relationship found in British theology. His early major work, *In Search of Foundations: English Theology: 1900–1920*, was the fruit of his lifelong study of English and Scottish theology and philosophy. The theology of grace found in these pages may be fairly described as "personalism" only if we understand personalism in British rather than Bostonian terms.

Early in Langford's theological development, he sought direction for an understanding of culture in Paul Tillich's theology. Langford always had the sense that God's grace had to be present in the midst of the fullness of life. And for a while, he was interested in Tillich's theology as a way to "correlate" God's grace and the realities of life. But the possibilities in Tillich's theology were soon abandoned as he set out his own. In Tillich he found questions and concerns that rightly arise from the reality of God's grace, but he found Tillich's "answers" were rooted in something other than God's grace as the gift of Godself in the form of Jesus Christ—the gift who draws us into relationship with God.

Because of his concern to proclaim the good news of grace to the contemporary culture, Langford was probably drawn to Tillich. But beyond a "theology of culture," Langford had an "evangelistic" intention. This intention and its shape were expressed in a reference that he made in every course that he taught and frequently in conversation as well. In chapter 1 of *Reflections on Grace*, Langford affirms the observation by Helmut Flender "that for Paul to say the same thing that Jesus said, it was necessary for him to say it in a different way." Langford then reveals his own commitment: "Such 'new saying' is always necessary. If this is so, how should we speak of grace in the tongue of our time?" This question of "missional fidelity" is a dominant concern in his theology.[10]

For Langford, finally, Tillich's theology, while committed to "new saying" did not convincingly answer "how?" because Tillich's theology of correlation is not shaped by Jesus Christ. In Langford's view, every

---

10. See Langford, *Practical Divinity*, 249, where he quotes C. K. Barrett, *Signs of an Apostle*, 50, who there refers to Helmut Flender, *St. Luke*, 163–67.

point of doctrine, whether it is about God, humankind, creation, sin, salvation, or any other, should be shaped by the grace received from Jesus Christ. Our new saying is not merely an expression of our experience; it is a witness to the God-centered, Christ-shaped grace that reconciles us to the God who is grace, yesterday, today, and tomorrow. Langford's lifelong interest in creative presence and the present, in new saying, is highlighted in his remark that, "to carry the cross means to carry what you learned at the cross."[11]

Grace comes to us differently through many means and shapes us differently in many ways. But it is always of God. We often become entangled in one definition or experience of grace and exclude all others from our teaching and life. Langford knew that such exclusion was wrong. We must recognize the very particular ways that grace comes to us and works in us, but to take that particularity for exclusivity is a theological error.

God-centered grace is generous grace. It is not without boundaries, but its redemptive work is accomplished as we are embraced by God's transforming power. As God seeks us, embraces us, and brings us into a transformative relationship, grace excludes nothing and changes everything.

Will Willimon notes in his foreword that Langford's faith was not the product of a revivalistic, violent conversion but the product of nurture and growth into Christian faith. He did not embrace one of these to the exclusion of the other but celebrated both—along with other means of God's grace. One of Langford's great insights into the history of theology and philosophy is that thinkers often erred not by affirming error but by denying truth.

Langford had an air of generosity that made him an indispensable member of the Duke University community during the civil rights upheavals and Vietnam War protests of the 60s and 70s. He was often a catalyst of mediation, reconciliation, and healing. Quite often, two people or two groups of people who could not trust each other found that they could both trust Tom Langford. The intelligent generosity that Langford brought to bear on such troubled occasions was not merely his way of restoring cordial pretense; instead, he believed

---

11. Taken from the address given at Greensboro College, October 8, 1996.

that the God he served had the power to change things for the better. However, Langford was well aware that because God's power is not coercive, no institution could expect to be continuously free of sin and spats of brokenness.

In Langford's theology, God is fully present in Jesus Christ. In him God fully embraces humankind; in him God is fully active to transform humankind. This fullness, however, does not mean that God is exhaustively or exclusively present in Jesus Christ. As we saw above in Langford's openness to dialogue with other religions, we do no service to God present in Jesus Christ by denying the presence of God's grace elsewhere or by restricting the presence of God's grace to Jesus Christ.

For the last hundred years or so, theologians have wrestled with the relationship between the knowledge of Jesus presented by the NT gospels and knowledge of Jesus that comes to us today. This relationship has been construed in a variety of ways. But in Langford's understanding, in the light of grace any gap between the biblical Jesus and how we know him today fades away. Because both the gospel writers and believers today know Jesus in the realm of grace and by grace, there is no significant distinction between the knowledge of Jesus proclaimed in the gospels and our knowledge today. The gospel writers knew Jesus by grace just as we also know him. Any supposed historical, cultural, ethical or metaphysical gaps must be acknowledged and dealt with, but they are insignificant when God is present, and the divine presence has not been withdrawn.

Calling the gospels "kerygmatized history," Langford wants us to see that both the gospel writers and present day believers are participants in human history graced by God's presence. The gospel writers proclaimed Jesus Christ as the one in whom and through whom they had been found by God's grace. For them as for us, there is no such thing as history understood apart from relationship to God in Jesus Christ. God-centered, Christ-shaped grace has become the thread that ties human history into a single, ongoing story.

In Langford's theology the encounter with God present spreads Christ-shaped grace out through the rest of life. Grace is not only most fully present in Jesus Christ, when it is present, it shapes its recipients in the image of Jesus Christ. Out of the generosity of transforming grace, we engage life as it comes to us in creation, in the realities of our world and in the disgrace of sin (see chapter 6) and its healing. In the light of grace, God is revealed and our lives are illuminated. We do not have to spurn grace in order to embrace life in all of its fullness and ambiguity. A theology centered in grace should not be constricted and desiccated, reducing and narrowing life. A theology of grace that is truly God-centered and Christ-shaped embraces all of life—its joys and sorrows, celebrations and sufferings, certainties and ambiguities, thanksgiving and confession. All of life is brought under the transforming power of grace that fulfills the desire of God for relationship beyond Godself.

Tom Langford lived this gracious embracing of life in its fullness. No area of life was strange to him. He delighted in sports as an athlete and fan. He enjoyed food, drink, art, and music. He enjoyed friendships with people across a broad spectrum of humanity. His most important human relationship was with his wife, Ann Marie, who shared life with Tom in its fullness and enriched its fullness with her poetry, homemaking, cooking, keen conversation, and warmth.

As a theologian in the Wesleyan tradition, Langford celebrated the *experience* of grace. Since grace is personal and relational, since it is God's life shared with us, grace is experiential. But in this turn to experience, Langford emphasized not just experience, but experience of *God*. Here he drew upon John Wesley, for whom "experience" meant "Christian experience." In continuity with Wesley, Langford opposed and corrected two extremes: those who claimed experience undisciplined by grace as a guide to theology; and those who had no place for experience in their theology. Because grace is personal, because it is being encountered by God present, a theology of grace cannot omit human experience.

Rooted in this understanding of the experience of grace, Langford radiated a piety that was far from pietistic. His piety was a this-worldly piety, not because he had capitulated to this world or abandoned hope in God, but because his knowledge of God's grace taught him that God is at work here and now—in this world and at this time. This piety was like second nature to him in his personal relationships and institutional efforts.

Although Langford develops a christocentric account of grace, he also commits himself to a trinitarian theology. Nonetheless, readers will notice that an explicit account of grace as the presence of the Holy Spirit is lacking. There may be several reasons for this omission. First, Langford became increasingly christocentric over the course of his career. Second, because he believed that grace *is* a person, that grace is Jesus Christ, his main concern was to ponder grace in personal terms. While Christians believe that the Holy Spirit is personal, what we have come to know of how God is personal derives from the life and teachings of the one who has been known—Jesus of Nazareth. Third, in the time that he had, Langford was more concerned with insights into the subject, what we have posthumously called *reflections on grace*, rather than creating a systematic work where all loose ends would be tied tightly together. But in any case, the incompleteness of the manuscript is evident here. Finally, in the God-centered and Christ-shaped account that we do have, the work of the Holy Spirit may possibly be detected or implied. Perhaps such indirection is appropriate to the Spirit's way of working. If that is what Langford intended, it is a pursuit well worth explicating more fully. And nothing in this manuscript prohibits or conflicts with such an explication of grace as the work of the Spirit.

We think that Langford would be untroubled by the incompleteness of his manuscript for at least two reasons. First, he knew that all human thought about God is incomplete. Second, in his own life and in his writing, he left room for others. Consider the following poem, which he wrote towards the end of his life:

YIELDING

Love may be expressed as yielding.
    Allowing space for another's weakness,
    Allowing space for another's strength.

Weakness may require accommodation,
    recognition of need,
    recognition of contribution,
    recognition of complementarity.

> To yield to weakness is an act of self-recognition,
> > As well as an act of recognition of another's ability
> > To contribute.
> > > True humility!
>
> Love also yields to another's strength.
> > Often a more difficult act;
> > > Initial response is to show more strength,
> > > Win the battle, establish one's greater power.
>
> To yield to strength requires that we acknowledge
> > Our own limitation, our own need of support.
>
> To yield is an act of humility,
> > Of affirmation and finding.
>
> Love is not self-sufficient.
> > Does not live independently from others;
> > > Does not play on another's weakness,
> > > > Does not deny another's strength.
>
> Love recognizes the weakness and strength of both
> > the one who gives and the one who receives.[12]

This poetic rumination is fitting with the kind of integrity that Langford possessed. It was not so much the kind of integrity that made people admire him, although some of that took place. Rather, it was a catalytic kind of integrity. He made those of us who know him want to do better in our own sphere of activity. It was community-fostering integrity.

Langford stresses (chapter 2) that God's act in Christ provokes a community forming, responsive presence in the body of Christ—in the church. God's presence invites and inspires us to become the sort of people and to do the sort of things that foster community. The church is a community of grace, and the means of grace that it typically presents, such as prayer, contemplation, *koinonia*, Bible study, and the sacraments of baptism and eucharist, encourage and invite further acts

---

12. Unpublished papers, dated March 22, 1998.

of responsive grace. *Reflections on Grace* is an incomplete work that we hope will invite completion by other members of the community. We think that further conversation, correction, and creative completion would have pleased Tom Langford.

CHAPTER ONE

Grace as Giver

*"Grace to you and peace from God the Father
and our Lord Jesus Christ."*

(Galatians 1:3)

God Present

God present is grace. God present to humankind is definitively expressed in the historical person of Jesus, the clearest expression of the character of God. In him is expressed God's intention and nature, God's mode and spirit of relating to human beings. God's being is expressed in this specific historical action in Jesus Christ; and as we allow the gospel to tell us who and what God is, we discover that God is gracious love.

Because this definition is not widely used, we need to say what we mean by this word *grace*. There are many options. For instance, in a published list of synonyms for *grace*, the following are given: the nouns *delicacy, tact, culture, courtesy, attractiveness, charm, compassion, mercy, saintliness,* and *piety*; and the verbs *to honor, to decorate,* and *to improve beauty and taste.* This is quite a list, but none of these synonyms goes to the heart of what Christians mean by *grace*.[1]

---

1. Paul uses the word "grace" (*charis*) approximately twice as many times as all of the rest of the New Testament authors. But Paul does not use the word we translate "grace" as a sharply defined concept or with a concern for theological consistency. To attempt to pin down Paul's usage would lead to a distortion. In this study, our use of "grace as Jesus Christ" is not an exact use following Paul's; rather, it is an extension of one aspect of Paul's thought, an attempt to be more systematic both in definition and

Within Christendom there has been a struggle over two basic understandings of grace. On the one hand, grace has been thought of as some *thing*, some thing God possesses and can give, and perhaps some thing persons can accept and possess; or, in larger terms, some atmosphere, energy, or power which represents God's action and provides a surrounding context for human life.

On the other hand, grace has been identified with some *one*; grace is a person, grace is God—God present to human beings. To speak of grace is to speak of God's presence and caring interaction with creation. In this understanding, considerations of grace are based upon reflections on the life, death, and resurrection of Jesus. Jesus Christ is grace; grace is Jesus Christ.

As a first consequence, grace is understood as God's particular initiating activity that draws human beings into covenant existence, an existence that finds expression in thankful worship of God and gracious service to neighbors. From this covenant vantage point, the reality of grace is recognized in a wide range of expressions, such as in the finding of truth, in the continuous act of creation, in the history of Israel, in the tension of grace with disgrace, in the church as a community of grace, and in Christian encounters with social structures.

Jesus Christ is the definitive but not the exclusive expression of grace. To see grace as God present in Jesus Christ prepares one to discover expressions of grace as the ubiquitous presence of God. From the perspective of grace given in Jesus Christ, receivers of grace become

---

in utilization of the concept. Consequently, as we present our thesis, it is done with an awareness of its partial support in New Testament discussions. See Manson, "Grace in the New Testament," 42–55. Quite opposite our own perspective, Cornelius Ernst, OP, argues, "But if my account has been even partially successful, it should be clear that Paul is using 'grace' to talk about a realm, a regime, an economy or dispensation, which in principle embraces all mankind. . . . 'Grace' is that order which is initiated by the sovereign generosity of God's self-giving manifested in the death and resurrection of Jesus Christ." See Ernst, *Theology of Grace*, 24.

The effort of our own study is to remove from the concept of grace the notions of "realm," "regime," "dispensation," or "order," and instead to understand grace as the relation of God to human beings—a direct, immediate giving of self to other selves. This self-giving is symbolized by special means of grace, but the "means" are completely secondary and not exhaustive of the working of grace. All God's dealings with human beings are expressions of an unrestrained and sovereign generosity of self-giving.

aware of grace in every activity of God. Hence, recognition of other forms of grace, whether anticipatory of Jesus's incarnation or resulting from it, depend upon our acknowledgment of this starting point: the definitive expression of grace is Jesus Christ.

The most basic character of grace is God's freedom, and its defining modality is God's free act of self-expression in human history. Grace as expressed in Jesus Christ is unnecessitated, surprising, and unforced. Grace is also a free act that liberates those whom it encounters. God meets human beings with forgiveness and renewal, and thereby creates new relationship. Bound by the love of Christ and unbound from all false loyalties, God's presence comes as claim and succor; this presence makes clear the meaning of both judgment and hope.

God's freedom is embodied in Jesus Christ. This historical person denotes who and what God is. Grace is not an abstract power, an impersonal quality, or a general ambience. God does not possess grace as an acquired or dispensable attribute. Because grace is not some thing God possesses and might give, grace is not a separable entity. God is grace in being and action; therefore, grace is a giver, not a gift. Grace is the character of divine life, and this character is known when divine life encounters human life as incarnate love manifest in the personal life of Jesus Christ.

To know grace, which is to know God, requires responsive faith, a faith which is graciously enabled. There is, in this sense, no theology of the unregenerate; the content of knowledge is conveyed through the positive relationship established by the encounter of God with human beings. Consequently, knowledge of grace comes in the experience of redemption by which God in Jesus Christ savingly encounters human beings and draws them into covenant. Such experience, while personal, is not individualistic; for the gospel of grace is conveyed through community, is nurtured in community, and is understood and interpreted by community. So God in Christ, working through the Holy Spirit, evokes a response of faith, and the established relationship sets the condition in which and through which grace is known.

The modes of grace's operation, as defined by the historical reality of Jesus Christ, are always personal. Care must be taken in using traditional expressions of the ways in which grace operates, such as "irresistible grace," "imputed grace," "imparted grace," "*sola gratia*," "predestination," and "election," to insure that both the integrity of God in Jesus Christ and the integrity of human beings, as displayed by Jesus Christ, are honored. Jesus Christ defines not only God's way of being in relation to persons but also the status of human beings in that relationship. That is, God meets human beings at eye-level. Human dignity is rooted in God's dignifying of human life through encounter by Jesus Christ. Human beings are respected and dealt with in ways that affirm both divine freedom and the integrity of human selfhood.

Grace as a person forms and is found in relationship. This relationship is the meaning of covenant. Grace is not an independent entity that works as an external force, nor is it exchanged through legal transaction. The paradigm of gracious activity is drawn from the realm of personal relationships. In the engagement of life, in being spoken to and answering, being addressed and responding, grace expresses its character. The God of grace is the One who engages and the One to whom responses can be made. Human life finds its meaning in this covenantal conversation. God's gracious presence creates and releases human capacity for relationship, for hearing and answering.

Grace as God's direct presence is quite distinct from grace as an ambience, as an attribute, as an abstract power, as an indwelling potentiality of nature, or as a divine endowment of human existence. Grace is God, the giving of God's self, God's way of being God, and God's way of being with us—Immanuel. Grace is God's self-giving for the purpose of establishing community.

Any interpretation of grace rests upon an understanding of the nature of the relationship between God and the created order, including human beings. Self-giving may utilize concrete media for expression, but self-giving emphasizes the one who is conveyed as well as the means of conveyance. Grace is God's offer of relationship, and in Jesus Christ, grace is God's direct self-offering. Relationship with God is the fundamental engagement in human life; it is the relationship which creates the meaning and purpose of life—covenant with God and one another.

In gracious relationship, we discern the basic nature of human relationships in which there is giving and receiving of person with person. Personal relationship involves intentionality, whether for good or evil, for mind–body engagement, for action, for mutual vulnerability and strengthening, or for mutual self-giving. Because personal relationship is engaging presence, no substitute token has more than an indicative or extrinsic value in the relation that is being offered. A gift of the self is not a discrete thing but the extending of one personal life to another that places oneself in relation to another, offering one's own being to another person. God's self-giving is the gift of God's own being, a gift which evokes responsive self-giving.

In gracious relationship we discern the nature of the triune God. Grace as the character of God is an expression of the Trinity, a focused act of corporate life. This fact has two primary implications. First, God's wholeness, the entire Trinity, presents itself in Jesus Christ. What is revealed in Jesus is true of the entire Godhead. Second, grace in human life is found in the bondedness of community with God and with other persons. From God's wholeness, life is maintained as whole in corporate existence. Consequently, grace expresses community and creates new community. Grace, as corporate and incorporating, establishes a new communal structure—the body of Christ.

The import of these claims is that grace is the distinctive element in the Christian message, for it is the most fundamental depiction of God, of God's way of being, and of human possibility. The range of grace is as comprehensive as God's relating to all creation. The expression of grace in Jesus Christ extends through the breadth, length, height, and depth of human experience. To be discovered by the grace of God in Jesus Christ leads to the possible discovery of the grace of God in creation, as prevenient presence, in present forgiveness, in maturing process, and in ultimate hope. Grace is the most permeative reality of Christian existence. God is present, and "in Him we live and move and have our being" (Acts 17:28).

A New Emphasis: Grace as Strength

What is the meaning of grace for our time? For Martin Luther, in the sixteenth century, the meaning was God's all-sufficient, unmerited love expressed as justification. *Sola gratia*, grace alone, was his cry, a cry that created one of those rare moments when a word changes a world. "Grace alone," he said, and nothing remained the same. Two centuries later, John Wesley spoke again of grace. Now the theme was enlarged: grace was understood as prevenient (acting for us before we are even aware of it), as forgiveness (justification), and as transformation of life (sanctification). Once again these words reverberated through a nation and then around the world. These powerful assertions shook the past and still echo through our time. But is it enough merely to repeat what we have received? Has grace already been adequately interpreted for all time? Can anything new be said? Can we remember and reinforce these themes from Luther and Wesley and then speak God's special work of grace for our era?

Helmut Flender, the New Testament scholar, has said that for Paul to say the same thing as Jesus said, it was necessary for him to say it in a different way. Such "new saying" is always necessary. If this is so, how should we speak of grace in the tongue of our time?

Grace is God's justifying and sanctifying presence. But what form is that grace taking in our world? Perhaps God's grace should be interpreted for our time as strength. Grace should be understood as God coming in justice, in judgment, in opposition to structured powers of evil, in challenge to all oppression, in standing by those in need.

To say that grace is strength is to recognize that we are dealing with a distinctive kind of power, a power for which there are no direct analogies in human experience, a power which can transform life by forgiving sin, by renewing existence, by remolding human forms of living. This power of grace is astonishing both in its being given and in what it accomplishes. The power of God to remake life is the first thing that must be said about strong grace.

The words *strong* or *strength* possess a variety of meanings. They may mean "having power to resist," "possessing large numbers of supporters," or "ability to effect one's decision." But *strong* may also mean "determined," "capable," or "not easily dissuaded or broken." This latter sort of strong grace engages persons in a determined, persistent, unfailing manner—as steadfast love. It engages social conditions with the strength to challenge, and to persist in its challenge, of demeaning, destructive conditions. Grace expresses deep empathy or antipathy as the situation requires.

Grace, as God present with us now, is strong love: God's caring and struggling where life is broken, abused, or denied. And grace makes us present with God. With God, we become servants of justice, defenders of the poor, challengers of culture, and critics of political and economic abuse. In these ways, we participate in God's coming kingdom.

A current understanding of grace may be pushed even further: the grace of God has corporate or systemic dimensions. For the grace of God incorporates us into the body of Christ, and thereby makes us aware of the connections of life, for we live within a web of relationships that shape societies. To be bound together in Christ makes us aware of the social bindings in which we live. Through Christ we discover the intrinsic connectedness of life in political, economic, and social dimensions of existence.

Recognition that life is cohesively bound in the body of Christ carries further recognition of the corporate character of all life. Hence, to seek justice, to feed the hungry, to care for the sick, to help the poor, and to release captives are Christian responsibilities because these are people whose lives are bound together with ours through Jesus Christ. By binding us into the body of Christ, God has also bound us together with all humankind and all creation.

Because grace possesses a corporate and incorporating character, God present may not be understood in individualistic terms; we are not each one related independently to God. God is certainly present with each person, but the presence of God also ties us together. When we pray "Our Father," we live in the body of Christ, so that every woman, man, and child—without exception—is our sister and brother to whom we are to be present.

Grace in our time, then, means what it meant to Luther and Wesley, but it also means God's presence as strength, a presence which comes with judgment and in opposition to embedded evil. The strong, incorporating presence of God binds us together in Christ and with the world. But what of the reverse truth, that grace may be present in weakness? There is a fundamental revelation of God as gracious in the crucifixion of Jesus, for God has come to the side of sinners and is self-giving even though this offer issues in rejection: "For our sake he made him to be sin who knew no sin, so that in him we might become the righteousness of God" (2 Cor 5:21). In this passage, grace is revealed in weakness.

What precisely is such weakness? Is the cross the only revelation of God's grace? The God who comes as willing subject to the powers of evil is one whose weakness evinces strength, even as with Paul, to use a human analogy, strength is revealed in weakness (2 Cor 12:9–10). Weakness is a form that strength may take—because it is strong enough to do so; it is the form strength takes in the cross. So the weakness of the cross, whereby God becomes subject to the forces of evil, is a self-chosen act; it is voluntary submission. When God allows the principalities and powers of this world to put to death, actually to kill, God's own incarnate act of self-giving, true strength becomes true weakness. Although destructive power overcame Jesus and put him in a tomb, the resurrection presents grace as strength. In raising Jesus from death, God demonstrates sovereign control over all creaturely conditions. Strength annuls the temporary victory of evil and proclaims the final triumph of God's providence. Grace expressed in the resurrection is strength. God's presence overcomes seeming defeat, and grace continues as strength in the ever-living Christ.

Grace comes in multiple forms, for God is present to every person and in every situation. There are no set patterns of how, where, or when God will be present. It may be by encounter, by succor, by challenge, by solicitous concern, by nurture or by judgment. God engages life as God wills and in response to particular human need, whether in political and economic arenas or in familial and personal areas. Grace as God's presence challenges, judges, and struggles. It perseveres, pursues, and presses as both demand and hope.

Understanding grace as a person renders the distinction between God's love for a sinner and God's hate for sin a false dichotomy. It is impossible to separate persons from their actions, for we express who we are in what we will, think, and do. God loves persons even when we sin, even as we are sinning. God so thoroughly loves the person, the sinner, that conversion and new personhood are possible.

How is the strength of grace actually used? Strength may be acceptably used to undergird, support, and enhance individual believers in personal relations and for support of existing social structures needing help. But should strength be used for civil disobedience, for challenge to established political or economic power, and for opposing structured expressions which hurt or misuse human beings?

To speak of grace as strength leaves open every exertion that comes from obedience to Jesus Christ as exemplified by his life and teachings and by his death and resurrection, and as authored by Christian community through study, prayer, and sensitive application of Christian ethical concern. It allows for sharp confrontation, for expressions of negative judgment, for organizing opposition, and also for suffering and self-surrender to oppressive powers.

If we take both Jesus's character and church history into account, any use of strength as political power or physical force is always subject to profound abuse and tyranny. Hence, any use of strength must be thoroughly self-critical and itself be subject to the judgment of grace. Strong action must first be humbled by the guiding sense of God present.

Grace is strength when God moves into a world distorted by group egoism, by political oppression, and by invidious control and economic exploitation. Into the actual human situation, God comes with grace—which means that God comes both like a refiner's fire and as gentle warmth.

Grace as strength is also expressed in systemic ways in the orders of social life. Some structures of society, whether family social units, voluntary groups or business organizations, or educational or church groups, are more just, more supportive, more conducive to freedom and maturation than are others. In every situation, grace seeks and supports a just ordering of social life.

Systemic arrangements are never static; consequently, good ordering does not retain value by inertia. On the contrary, valuable structures must continually be adjusted and readjusted in order to remain valuable; social arrangements must continually be reset according to the goals sought. In social and individual arenas, grace must correct as well as confirm.

Illustrations of grace as strength may be seen in the reinterpretation of some traditional virtues. Christian virtues have sometimes been described as weak, passive, or yielding. Reinterpretation is needed to capture their full character. For instance, patience, which is usually thought of as enduring, "putting up with," or as being self-effacing, may also be interpreted as remaining firm in the service of a good cause, as refusal to surrender, or as tenaciously standing for what is right. Again, humility is often thought of as the negation of self-claiming, as willingness to be used, or as passive acceptance of conditions; but humility may also be interpreted as placing a person or a cause before one's own self-interest, as willingness to do good without reward, or as striving selflessly for justice. Gentleness is often thought of as meekness or mildness, as moderateness or lack of drive, but gentleness may also be interpreted as strength so controlled that it can touch without increasing pain, as ability to hold off without bruising, as capacity for completing graciously what has been started—even in social or communal settings. Such gentleness may be understood as an expression of strength.

Grace as strength must, for our time, also be extended into areas of human conflict. How could grace stand apart from those places where life is most in tension? God as grace is at those places where people maim and kill one another; God is present where human love is absent. God is where people starve and are sick, where people are homeless and emotionally lost; God is present in the slum and the refugee camp. God sides with people in special need. This means that God is also judgmentally present in the boardroom, in the executive council, in the political conference, among the "power brokers," in the strategy meeting, listening to the CEOs, presidents, and cabinet members.

Revolt Against Grace

There is a modern revolt against the idea of grace, against the power of God present, and against the notion of human need for grace. This revolt extends from Renaissance humanism through the Enlightenment's social planning, technological manipulation, and psychological theories of self-realization. For these traditions, human beings must be independent, capable of self-construction and self-reconstruction, and individually responsible for the achievement of meaning in their personal and social lives. Consequently, contemporary sensibility can negatively react to the idea of grace as God present for human need. To speak of grace sounds like a feudal remainder, reminiscent of fixed hierarchy, with its dependence upon the unpredictable good will or predictable self-interest of another person of superior status. Grace is, in this understanding, expressive of an attitude of condescension. It emphasizes control by a superior and alien power; at best it expresses *noblesse oblige*. Such an interpretation sets grace in contrast to the human right for psychological and political self-control, to a legitimate, independent status, and to responsibility for a just order. Contemporary people do not want or need to live by the grace of others; there are firmer, more self-dependent, more predictable foundations upon which life may be established. Helmut Gollwitzer, in turn citing Johann Gottfried Seume, expresses a dominant modern attitude: "No good, upright, reasonable man will wish to be saved by grace, not even if a dozen evangelists say so."[2]

Likewise, in *Bread and Wine* Ignatio Silone tells the story of an Italian revolutionary who disguises himself as a priest. Under pressure to maintain his disguise, he offers a woman absolution. And she, out of appreciation, insists on making him a gift of a chicken. The priest refuses to accept the gift: "Grace costs nothing," he says. In anger, she responds, "There is no such thing as free grace." To conclude the argument, she throws the chicken on the table and runs away.[3]

Similarly, Richard Rorty has pronounced a contemporary judgment: "Once grace, salvation, and the Divine Nature were subjects of study; now the fact that they were so is a subject of study."[4] Rorty's assessment gives pause. Is the study of grace truly passé? May life be described and lived as well without as with grace? In spite of these objections, we proceed because the encounter with grace evokes reflection on grace. The ascription of primacy to grace is not the expression

2. Gollwitzer, *Introduction*, 167.
3. Silone, *Bread and Wine*, 83.
4. Rorty, *Consequences of Pragmatism*, 32.

of one option among others; it is a response required by the actual formation of life by grace—by God present.

For contemporary persons, self-sufficiency or independence often means nonindebtedness. Self-valuing status is derived from not being dependent upon or obligated to others. The claim of rights, the right to life, the right to liberty, to happiness, and the like, which is legitimate and necessary for human construction of social and political systems, is given universal and total application, even ontological status. Self-control means not to be owing, not to have to say "thank you." The extension of independence to freedom from God constitutes a common contemporary attitude and intention.

The Breadth of Grace

But for those who live by grace, God present sets the context for the interpretation of life. The Greek word for grace, *charis*, is derived from the root *char*, "that which brings joy." Grace, as an act and invitation, is a gift that evokes gratitude. With delight we are engaged by the self-giving God, and so we proclaim the joyous message of grace.

God's grace is an expression of God's nature as agape. It is God coming to humankind in love, with forgiveness, with affirmation, with challenge. Grace is God sharing human life, identifying with human experience in such a way as to create the possibility of covenant, of a community of life. In order to initiate covenant, the Creator comes to human beings, participates in our existence, and continues with us as guide, companion, judge, and Lord. In its covenantal intention, the gospel of "grace and truth" given in Jesus Christ expresses both God's character and God's intention for human life.[5]

In Jesus Christ, God's grace is a constant and comprehensive presence. As such, the experience of grace must not be reduced to Pollyanna moments; to things working to our advantage; to affirmations of abundance, privilege, or enclosed self-interest. Grace is experienced and expressed through God present in everyday moments of ordinary life, in times of both joy and disappointments in relationships,

---

5. See Jeremias, *Central Message*, 84.

in times of renewed strength as well as fatigue, and in the warmth of human love as well as in periods of indifference.

Focusing on grace does not minimize or trivialize the reality of evil. In the cross, evil is recognized for its enduring strength and destructive power. Grace sees evil and confronts it; divine presence takes sides in titanic struggle with unrighteousness.

Grace has an edge. God is not present simply as rounded curves and encompassing acceptance. Grace is neither the absence of judgment nor infinite compassion. Rather, grace is the sharpness of God engaging human conditions. It is God's presence as strength in struggle, as denier of evil, as opponent of exploitation. Grace has an edge, a well-tempered edge like a surgeon's scalpel, an edge used for healing, an edge which cuts to make healing possible.

Grace must be kept in tight tension with atonement, for only as grace and atonement are viewed together does grace retain its strength. God present and acknowledged is atonement. Grace unidentified with atonement slips into vapid sweetness and cheap affirmation. Grace as atonement confronts and struggles with evil. Grace is a cross and a crossing-over; it is self-giving to the extent of suffering. In the cross of Jesus Christ, love and justice, strength and vulnerability, are bound together in suffering love. The gracious God becomes sin in order to overcome sin. God is the loving judge, who, as grace, looks squarely at evil and condemns it, and who, as grace, looks squarely at the condemned and forgives. Atonement removes the possibility of proclaiming cheap grace. Grace is costly to God, as costly as death, and grace is costly in its demand for gracious response and responsibility.

Grace bestows life by creating new relationship. The divine act of creation calls forth human life and enhances human creativity. Grace is God's gift of shared life, a gift given to be expressed through human acts. "Gracious life" is life reflective of God's way of being in Jesus Christ; it is human life expressing, in broken partiality, the quality and character of Jesus's being for other people; it is the creative and fresh expression of self-giving for neighbors.

Grace is embodied in concrete sharing of life with life; it is as real as the conditions in which life must be lived. In the cross, the reality of grace encounters the reality of the world; God's grace meets human disgrace. The cruciform grace of God was planted in the earth of human existence and continues to confront the hurt and meanness of human life. God's cruciform grace is also hunger-formed, forgiveness-formed, and peace-formed; it is poverty-formed, fidelity-formed, and justice-formed. Graciousness possesses the vulnerability of radical caring and the tenacity of steadfast loyalty; graciousness possesses a capacity for identification with alienated and excluded people, and a willingness to take sides in the service of God's good will. As Gerard Manley Hopkins has seen, God's creativity engages and directs human creativity:

> I say more: the just man justices;
> keeps grace: that keeps all his goings graces;
> Acts in God's eye what in God's eye he is—
> Christ—for Christ plays in ten thousand places,
> lovely in limbs, and lovely in eyes not his
> To the Father through the features of men's faces.[6]

Through Jesus Christ, life is graced, and the rule of God has been inaugurated and reaches toward consummation. Graced life is life reaching toward its true goal of life in God. God's sovereignty is expressed as love that calls faithful people to responsive love and disposes them in the service of gracious struggle. The coming of new life upon the old order always meets with resistance, sometimes with striking defeat—as in the cross of Christ. Yet, grace is strong and tenacious; it does not stop being itself.

The Wonder of Grace

In contemplating grace, we come not to comprehension but awe. Throughout Christian history, grace has been described as divine extravagance, a description rightly required by fidelity to the subject matter. Grace is extravagant because it goes beyond reasonable, prudential, or expected limits, because it moves beyond ordinary bounds of human action or love. Grace is extravagant as God's gracious love is extravagant, as the cross is extravagant, as the resurrection is ex-

---

6. Hopkins, "As Kingfishers Catch Fire," lines 9–14.

travagant. As grace, God is most distinctively God, most extravagantly God.

The sheer unexpected, unclaimable effusiveness of God's grace is the cause of wonder, amazement, awe. As we review the character of the embodiment of grace in Jesus Christ, we become aware of the awesome character of God's action. And we are made humbly reverent when engaged by the extravagant love of divine life. The path of reflection on the theme of grace leads to wonder—that which everyone who has experienced grace knows but no one can adequately express. Our language falls short, but knowing more than we can say, we must say what we can in order to further extend what we might know about God who is grace.[7]

---

7. For us, the specific relation of grace to Jesus Christ is most basic. Luther affirmed this identification, as did Calvin. John Wesley was consistently clear that the normative expression of God's grace is Jesus Christ and that the most adequate Christian interpretation of grace is reflection on that unique event. More recently, Karl Barth and Karl Rahner, made the gracious event of Jesus Christ central in their theological systems. To explore theological meaning by means of the theme of grace is a continuation of an ongoing theological perspective which we honor by attempting fresh restatement.

CHAPTER TWO

Grace and Truth

*And the Word became flesh and dwelt among us, . . .
full of grace and truth.*

(John 1:14)

Grace as God present creates Christian presence in the world. Grace is creative of new existence; to know grace is to be gracious. Knowledge is related to truth, and truth is an expression of one's status in relation. A formula makes the point: God's presence is true; human response is a reach for truthful understanding and action. This reach for truth defines human faithfulness; human faithfulness is alignment with God as true. This being and knowing dynamic defines grace as received and defines grace as expressed.

God as True and Truth

There is a direct relationship between grace and truth. For God is true, and grace is God present to all creation eliciting responsive presence. Positive relationship, when established, produces both interaction and conformity of life with life. First, grace is God's conforming identification through divine condescension with fallen creation (Phil 2:5–11). Such conformation is a double transformation: God is transformed as the Word became flesh (John 1:14); and creation is transformed as misalignment is reordered into conformation with God (John 1:12; Rom 12:2).

God, who is true, graciously reconciles creation, including human creatures, with God's self; as a result, that which had lost its true relation is reclaimed into positive alignment or covenant. God as true sets life truly. This re-creating relationship establishes life as true and gives rise to truthful expression.

The classical definition of theology as faith seeking understanding reflects this point, especially when faith is understood as the graciously enabled response to grace. Faith, understood in this way, is not merely intellectual assent, singular affection, or separable obedience. Faith is not reducible to belief, feeling, or act. Faith is the holistic response of persons to the full self-giving of God. Faith is a way of being, a mode of existence.

Life as faith gives rise to faithful reasoning, faithful trust, and faithful obedience. A part, and only a part, of holistic faith is faithful reasoning. Reason, or theological endeavor arising from the true alignment of life, reflects upon the source and condition of that true existence.

Grace and truth are bound together in Jesus Christ—the expression of God's glory. This combination and congruence of terms is of course found in the Prologue of the Gospel of John where "glory," "grace," and "truth" are said to have come "through Jesus Christ" (John 1:16–17). This New Testament account recalls the Old Testament passage, where God, whom no one can see and survive, "appears" to Moses and "shows" the divine glory to Moses. This Lord is said to be "merciful and gracious, slow to anger and abounding in steadfast love and faithfulness, keeping steadfast love for thousands, forgiving iniquity and transgression and sin, but who will by no means clear the guilty" (Exod 34:6–7).

In the Gospel of John, "steadfast love and faithfulness" are translated into "grace and truth."[1] The reference to Exodus stresses the contrast made by the Gospel of John between the partial, previous human knowledge of God and the definitive disclosure of God in the incarnation. Jesus Christ, as grace and truth, creates life in conformity with his own life.

Hanson notes that Paul less explicitly but similarly argues that when Moses "sees" God's glory, he will discover that God is a God of mercy (Rom 9:14–16). Paul draws the christological conclusion "that

---

1. See Hanson, *Grace and Truth*, 6–7.

Christ became a servant . . . to show God's truthfulness, in order to confirm the promises given to the patriarchs, and in order that the Gentiles might glorify God in his mercy" (Rom 15:7–9).[2] Hanson carries this theme of mercy on to the relation of Matthew 9:13 and 12:7 to Hosea 6:6; he finds the same emphasis on mercy in Luke and in the Pastoral Epistles.

In the Old Testament, steadfast love and faithfulness are conveyed by God's covenant character; in the New Testament, grace and truth are conveyed in the career of Jesus. And these qualities establish the condition for being "in Christ." To be in Christ is to be included in the grace, truth, and life of Christ that give rise to expressions of human graciousness and truthfulness.

God's glory, manifest in Jesus Christ, is, through Christ, manifested in human existence. True human existence is truly shaped by God's glory and is expressive of God's glory. That is, conformation to Jesus Christ is the authentic sculpting of human existence. In human life that participates in the body of Christ, there is refracted glory, and the invisible God is, in modulated form, expressed in the graciousness of human self-giving. God's glory is made known as the body of Christ is given for the world.

The effulgence of grace is Jesus Christ, whose glory both reveals God and is revealed through human faithfulness. The primary point of reference is the Word who became flesh. The relation of the true God to the truth of God is mediated through Jesus Christ who is truth.

Grace as Praxis

Truth is not to be understood in an exclusively intellectualistic sense, for it is not reducible to cognitive categories. Rather, *truth* refers to the conformity of life to Jesus Christ, and this conformity is inclusive of mind, heart, and hands. Truth is known through living which is inclusive of thought, affections, and service.

The interpretation of grace as praxis must be carried through with thoroughness. Truth refers to truthfulness of life lived "in Christ" and in conformity to Christ. As such, it includes intellectual construction

2. Ibid., 12–13.

of truthful statements but only as a part of a whole life that is truly aligned to God through worship, a whole life that is lived in faithfulness to God through love of neighbor. Theological search is not for abstract truth but for that which transforms human living. Praxis is the context of lived existence within which theory is developed; practice designates the application of previously developed theory.

Truth, in this discussion, is not located in technical or controlling reason. It is not the type of reason which allows the one who knows to manipulate or utilize aspects of reality. Rather, truth is reason as wisdom, reason that comes out of and serves living relationship. It is knowledge that arises from and serves the transformation of life.

Stephen Toulmin has argued that philosophy since the seventeenth century has been dominated by a "theory centered style, which poses philosophical problems, and frames solutions to them, in timeless and universal terms."[3] By doing this, Toulmin claims these philosophers left half of the subject "languishing." That is, the practical dimensions of thought-life or living-thought were unattended to, and what was lost were spheres of thought such as the "oral," the "particular" the "local," and the "timely."[4] Certainty rather than wisdom was the goal. But this dominant understanding of reason must be challenged. The recovery of practical philosophy, of praxis theology, is a paramount task that signals the transformative effect of wisdom keenly aware of social location. Specifically, this means that doctrines are not ends in themselves but are guidelines that help us to know how to tell the story of God's grace rightly and to live it with integrity.

The incarnate form of God's truthful self-expression is truthful life. Grace operates in actual historical frames of existence as God becomes incarnate, at a definite time and place with its own set of social conditions. As grace operates historically, it gives rise to innovative discipleship in definite times, places, and social conditions. The knowledge of God is knowledge that arises within and is lived out in a specific social location. The truth of God is truth expressed—always in incomplete ways—through life formation. To be "in Christ" is to be in the relationship that makes such knowledge—such life forma-

---

3. Toulmin, "Recovery," 338.
4. Ibid.

tion—possible: the Christ form of God's truthful self expression gives rise to formation in Christ of Christian existence.

God present, God as grace, is a mystery both in regard to the origin of its expression in God's freedom and in regard to its character in God's self-giving; God always remains both hidden and revealed. God's freedom, will, and character are known definitively but not exhaustively in Jesus Christ.

The mystery of grace stands before us as blinding light, as the effulgence of glory, as the cloud of unknowing. Yet that light also shines in the face of Jesus Christ (John 1:9; 1 Cor 4:5). That which human beings have no capacity to see is now seen. That which comes as blinding darkness also burns away the opaque shrouding of our eyes. Jesus, who is truth, opens for us the possibility of recognizing and acknowledging truth. Human incapacity for truth, as true loving, thinking, and serving, is graciously recapacitated for knowing the truth who is Jesus Christ. But human knowledge of truth is not a direct reflection of him who is grace and truth. For Christ is also a mystery in which truth is both revealed and hidden. Truth is revealed through the truing of life, and, as a consequence, through understanding God, the world, and human existence from the newly created mode of being.

The truth known through Jesus Christ arises from being captured by the one who is truth. Therefore, the initial move toward truth is to love him who is truth. The love of truth, the worship of God, is the commanding reality which makes possible its discovery and expression. The love of God, not the control of truth or the correct expression of truth, is the motivation and goal of Christian truth seeking and truth speaking. To be possessed by truth, not to possess truth, characterizes Christian existence. Thus truth arises from a way of being, from a mode of relationship.

The Johannine theme of knowing the truth by doing the truth points in the correct direction. Knowing the truth and doing the truth are both expressions of being in relation to the One who is true and truth. Faith is presented in the forms of life itself. How does the truth of Christian confession, intellectually formulated, relate to the truth that is Jesus Christ? How do the contents of creeds relate to the character of Jesus Christ? How do faithful statements of truth relate to God's living expression of truth?

At the most, human statements of Christian truth are analogies, metaphors, or pointers to the truth of Christ. Truthful being cannot completely capture Christ, and truthful statements cannot probe the depths of grace. We may know God truly but not exhaustively. But what is the nature of such "true" knowing? To pursue this question, we must once again follow a distinctive track, a track rather different from our usual, western point of beginning.

Communal Truth

To be "in Christ" is the condition of being true and of knowing truth, and this is corporate existence. Consequently, truth, in Christian terms, is not primarily an individual acquisition, attainment, or discovery. Truth possesses a communal context and is produced through communal interaction, correction, and agreement.

Truth arises out of life in community. In keeping with the biblical, corporate sense of Christian existence, and in contrast with Enlightenment rationality and individualism, truth is conveyed through community, i.e., in covenant. The ordering of life with God within the company of believers sets the dimensions of true human existence. Hence, it is within community and as community that the search for truth occurs. One way of making this emphasis is to draw a distinction between persons in community and the community of persons, that is, to stress the communal formation of personal life as more primary than the movement of persons into community. Corporate personhood is the reality of Christian existence. The community of persons, whose life is lived as the body of Christ, is the presupposition of true living and truth finding.

Truth also reflects communal consensus. Truth is not individual discovery by persons who are only loosely connected to a covenant community. Rather, personal existence, including search for and statement of truth, is communally formed. Consequently, this corporate theme emphasizes the importance of creeds and doctrinal standards that represent communal consent.

Such standards convey the foundational convictions of concrete historical traditions as these have been developed, critically assessed, and accepted as the primary statements of Christian communal self-identity.

At the same time, it must be clearly acknowledged that there are multiple communal understandings of Christian truth. There are great varieties of Christian tradition, different dogmatic developments, distinct doctrinal emphases, and contrasting creedal formulations. Consequently, appeal to a communal ethos of truth is not to claim that there is a single tradition of corporate Christian truth that overrides individual Christian interpretations. The diversity of Christian traditions reinforces the necessary modesty of all Christian theological assertions. The variety of communal truth traditions manifests the partiality of all claims to human possession of truth.

In spite of the lack of finality of truth claims by any human tradition, it is important to achieve the relatively higher ground of corporate truth claims over private, idiosyncratic, theological affirmations. Corporate bodies can be parochial, narrow-minded, self-protecting and malformed. Hence, corporate bodies also require self-critical evaluation. And, for Christian community, the status of being "in Christ" should be, even though it not always is, the commanding reality that brings every community under judgment of the lordship of Jesus Christ, of the valid claims of other communities of Christian faith, and of the sinful presumption of exclusive possession of divine truth.

God present creates life as covenant communal formation; such formation is the context of Christian life and its conveyance as true and truthful understanding of God. The truth so gained is wisdom about the truing of life and of the implications of true life for truthful interpretation.

There is a history of different understandings of the relation of Christian truth understanding to the truth expressed in Jesus Christ. Traditions have variously emphasized dogmatic, intellectual statements; personal, existential appropriation of truth meaning; cultural shaping of truth claims; or ethical consequences of belief systems. But our starting point and emphasis is participation in the life of God, concretely expressed through being "in Christ," mediated through concrete community to the end of loving, thinking, and serving as expressions of this mode of existence. At most, we can claim that intellectual truths constitute a wisdom about life truly established and focused by grace.

Church: Community of Grace

Community is established by God present and responded to. The church, as a community of grace, is the historical embodiment of realized relationship. Hence, Christian life is life "in Christ," life bound together in corporate existence. Life "in Christ" represents the truing of life with God; in Christian community, we live in "right" relationship with God.

Protestant evangelism and pietism, by stressing individual salvation and personal relation to God, has made Christian community adjunctive and secondary. But Christian life is life in community. Christian existence is nurtured, shaped, sustained, and guided in and by gracious community. Life in a community of grace is life lived in conformity with God.

There are three chief emphases to be found in this understanding: the corporate origins of Christian existence, in which prevenient grace brings about incorporating presence; the corporate content of Christian existence, the means of grace; and the corporate hope of Christian existence as eschatological community.

Prevenient Grace as Incorporating Presence

Prevenient grace, as proffered presence, is temporally prior as both past and future. As Creator and consummator, as source and succor, prevenient grace establishes Christian existence as corporate. God present is alpha and omega, who, as active presence, constitutes the possibility and actuality of community.

The universality of prevenient grace, as redemptive intention, is known from the perspective of Jesus Christ. In Christ, God's saving intention for all creation is made evident. This theological claim is not undisputed. A long history in Christian theology has spoken of a limited atonement and of a radical separation between those redeemed and those rejected. And there is no final, undebatable answer to the question of God's universal intention for the salvation of all creation. But it is reasonable to draw upon the numerous (but not exclusive) New Testament passages that emphasize God's ubiquitous presence as redemptive intention (Eph 1:9–10; Col 1:15–19; Phil 2:9–11). It is reasonable to extend the love of God made evident in Jesus Christ to be inclusive of all creation.

The initiative of God's love as exhibited in Jesus Christ is the foundation of our understanding: "While we were yet sinners, Christ died for us" (Rom 5:8); and, "We love him because he first loved us" (1 John 4:19). God's reach for humankind is prior to any human reach for God; thus prevenient grace points to God as Creator, whose free creative will is the gracious source of all creation and of all covenant relationship.

God as Creator does not point simply to the past or to origination alone, for God's creative activity is continuous; it is also present and future activity. God was present, is present, and will be present. God's presence is creative origin for all that has been, all that is, and all that will be. Prevenient grace is continuous, ongoing presence. When we confess, "Jesus Christ, the same yesterday, today and forever" (Heb 13:8), we also affirm the continuity of prevenient grace through the total range of time.

Prevenient grace is incorporating presence, for the previousness, the beforehandedness, of God invites into community. God present invites responsive presence in the body of Christ. Prevenient grace is hope, for God who "goes before" leads into the future. Drawn by the presence of God in Jesus Christ, Christian response is, through Christ and in Christ, participation in the always-present life of God. The reality of prevenient grace means that all of creation is graced, that all of life is lived by and in God present.

Life as graced is life together in covenant, and life together in covenant is new creation. Graced life is holistic (holy) existence; it is continuous re-creation of human existence in relation to God and human community. Such new creation requires fresh creative activity by God. God's presence creates the redemptive present, the present that is constituted by the presence of God and the newly given covenant neighbor.

Prevenient grace—God's universal, seeking presence—is responded to and witnessed to by the body of Christ; indeed, through its response and witness, the church is the body of Christ. The church, as the congregation of the called, through its worship and koinonia, embodies the response to grace. The reach of the church, as the congregation in mission, embodies through its service a witness of grace. Hence, prevenient grace is incorporating presence that draws into covenant.

To speak of prevenient grace often conveys a sense of passive acceptance, of weakness before God, and an assertion of human inability. But prevenient grace expresses the strength of grace, of God's free initiation, persevering faithfulness, vulnerable strength as inviting presence, continual struggle with evil, and unfailing support of righteousness. Prevenient grace is not simply a presupposition or a condition of creation. Prevenient grace is God willfully, sustainingly present. As God's way of being, grace is God's decision to be present to all creation.

Means of Grace as Corporate Content

As grace creates community through shared presence, the formation of a community should be thoroughly imbued with grace in its shaping of relationship, lifestyle, and liturgy. Every aspect of existence is rooted in grace and strives to embody the reality of God present.

Historically the church has found the presence of God (which may be expressed when, how, and where God freely wills), to be ordinarily expressed through particular means. There is no fixed list of these means, but among those most frequently mentioned are prayer, Bible study, preaching, Christian fellowship, baptism, and the Lord's Supper. As a community of grace, the church finds its vitality as God's presence is communicated and directly engaged through these concrete media.

While forms of worship represent prevailing emphases, as do devotional forms and understandings of mission, no conclusive argument for one emphasis over another can be directly drawn from the reality of God present. Yet, as we emphasize that grace is a giver and not a gift, we can also ask, how is God present functioning in the means of grace?

Means of grace are the media by which God engages human life. They are neither necessary nor exclusive, in the sense that God must work through these specific means, or that God's presence cannot be known outside of these means. But these means do represent significant ways through which Christian community with God has been realized, and they are therefore honored, utilized, and nurtured. Obviously, this has been so with prayer, and prayer is perhaps the most "ordinary" of the means of grace.

Prayer

To pray is to respond to the presence of God. Prayer takes place because we have been invited by grace, because we are encountered by God present. By grace we have been spoken to; by grace we can answer. Prayer is living in the presence of God. In this presence we make no stipulations; set no requirements; find no room for manipulation; and make no calculus of power, influence, or success. Through grace, we are invited into shared life, and we know the urgency of this invitation by Jesus's life, death, and resurrection.

Prayer is possible only because of grace, which moves the holy God to humanity's side. Only grace overcomes both reverent fear of God's holiness and unholy fear of alienation from God. Only grace addresses humanity with such forgiveness and strength, with such acceptance and affirmation as to make response possible. To pray is to participate in the life of God. Prayer is the language of covenant; it comes out of and reflects the actuality of community.

Response to God present may be spoken; indeed, "speaking with God" is the most common expression of shared life. Meditation or "thinking with God" in order to explore, appreciate, or understand is also an authentic means of living in the Presence. Contemplation, "being with God," deeply and immediately accepts and affirms God's presence. In every form, prayer is practicing the presence of God.

Presence calls forth presence, as divine/human encounter takes on a primary form in prayer.

Prayer is being with God who is with us. In relationship centered in the presence of God, life is found, community is discovered, and the entire range of existence is shared. As a means of grace, prayer actualizes God's self-presenting and human acknowledgment.

Bible Study

Bible study is also an ordinary means of grace because the Bible can be the media of God's encounter with human beings. The Bible, as the story of God's activity, makes past history present. As it conveys God's activity, biblical history can become as much a present reality as one past. Under the aegis of the Holy Spirit, the reading of Scripture can establish the possibility for God to speak and to be heard.

Linguistic study, critical historical awareness, and literary interpretation all contribute to readiness to read the biblical text. But all these are prolegomena for the Scripture to function as scripture. For Scripture to be a means of grace it must convey the presence of God. Prayers of illumination before the reading of Scripture in services of worship recognize this dynamic as they petition that hearts be prepared so that the worshippers may hear what God has to say.

Fellowship

The koinonia or fellowship found in Christian community is also a means of God's presence creating a time and space of presence with God and with other worshippers. Prayer, like Bible study, is profoundly corporate. Participation in life bound together in Christian community, as a reflection of God's binding presence, embodies the incorporating nurture of grace and provides a dynamic witness to grace.

Here, as in all of the other means, realized presence points to the profundity of what it means to be "in Christ" and what it means to say that one's life is hidden with Christ in God (Col 3:3). Grace shares itself as community and is embodied as gracious presence with one another. Grace and responsive faith create, in Charles Williams's language, "coinherence," a living in and through one another.[5] The actualization of this coinherence is the fruiting of grace in the body of Christ.

Baptism

While much more can be said of the sacrament of baptism, "God present" is its central theme. Beyond this core many different practices and interpretations have been built, oftentimes with conflicting interpretations, but no formula or specified acts command the presence of God. As with all of the other means, baptism is a mode of conveyance that God may and does freely use to convey self-presentation. By gracious allowance, God offers to believers the privilege of participating in this means of grace. Whatever else baptism might mean in empirical exemplifications of community, it enacts God's prevenient presence and represents the reality of actualized covenant.

Eucharist

The chief means of grace, and the central sacrament, is the Lord's Supper. Here the presence of God comes to sharpest focus and to its most explicit enactment: "This is my body"; "This is my blood." Here all of our themes join together: God present in Jesus Christ is received through participation and results in new being in covenant.

The word *Eucharist* is built around the core of grace (*charis*). It represents grateful acknowledgment of grace given, thankful joy for grace received, gracious acceptance of graceful gift. The act of Eucharist affirms: "I am crucified with Christ, nevertheless I live, yet not I, but Christ lives in me" (Gal 2:20; KJV slightly altered). In every means of grace, God's presence is conveyed, and through this conveyance the reality of the church as a community of grace is actualized.

In sum, means of grace must also be interpreted in terms of God's presence as strength. There is a persistent tendency in western Christianity to privatize Christian existence, but the means of grace presuppose corporate existence. Conveyance by the ordinary means

---

5. For a full development of the concept of coinherence, see Williams, *Descent of the Dove*.

through community represent God's faithful presence and embodiment of divine/human relationship. This embodiment is in the midst of actual human conditions and therefore comes as challenge, judgment, new hope, and reconciliation. The means of grace do not separate us from the world so much as they engage us with the world. They do not so much support private piety as they extend our piety into the public contexts of church and world. Grace as strength is conveyed through ordinary means that shape Christian existence.

Grace as Eschatology

Life "in Christ," within the reign of God, is life which has found its present significance in gracious presence, and which anticipates ultimate hope for full covenant. God present is alpha and omega, for grace extends from prevenience to consummation. Grace confronts creation with both realized eschatology and anticipated fulfillment.

God present dynamically challenges human existence with judgment and reconciliation. Grace is often misinterpreted as simply being affirming or accepting, and ultimately affirmation and acceptance may be the divine intention. But the strength of grace is often initially evident as the eschatological thrust of judgment. To be confronted by God who is righteous evokes a sense of unrighteousness: "I saw the Lord . . . and I said 'Woe is me'" (Isa 6:1, 5). Realized eschatology is the present in-breaking of God's judgment as well as God's reconciliation.

To meet the living God can impel a desire to escape. The sheer wonder of holiness creates a sense of the inappropriateness of presumption that one should be present with God. But the presence of holiness also creates a sense of misalignment. How can unrighteousness stand before divine goodness? The stress upon the corporate and incorporating character of grace presses the issue into the arena of systemic structures and social order: God's presence challenges evil social structures. God as true commands true ordering of life; God present engages human structures as judgment upon all denials of what grace represents and intends. Hence, denials of human freedom, justice, peace, ecological well-being, and spiritual opportunity are to be judged, opposed, and fought.

Grace comes as succor of the hungry, the homeless, the poor, and the oppressed; it is succor of the deprived, the marginal, and the disenfranchised. Grace also comes as succor to the spiritually impoverished and to those who deny community and reject relationship. But presence as total engagement does not separate neatly between the physical, social, and spiritual dimensions of life. Responsive relationship with God may be formed in any social, economic, or political condition, but the presence of God challenges those conditions which thwart full-orbed response and responsibility.

Strong grace, God present as strength, cuts against typical understandings of grace as passive acceptance of the status quo and opposes the power of evil in the name of goodness. Grace does not disguise or hide actual hurt; it does not overlook or blink at the reality of destruction. Rather, grace is self-offering that moves into destructive arenas, stands against evil, identifies with brokenness, and fights for reconciliation.

Ultimately grace seeks reconciliation. God present represents culminating eschatological hope, but this hope comes through the winnowing of judgment. Denial of God's presence as commanding justice represents false understanding. There are consequences that grace opposes, some that grace can correct, but also some that grace must annul rather than reconcile.

Judgment is an expression of grace, a consequence of gracious presence. Rehabilitation rather than punitive vengeance is its character. As a consequence of this rehabilitative character, grace encounters, challenges, and judges with the intention of rectifying injustice and destructive power.

But there remains a final vision of God as all in all. Grace remains grace—steadfast, unfailing, and unconquerable. And grace offers the ultimate hope that God is present, always present: "The kingdom of the world has become the kingdom of our Lord, and of his Christ, and he will reign for ever and ever" (Rev 11:15).

CHAPTER THREE

Grace and the Biblical Jesus

You believe in grace, Porphyry.... Oh, had you but recognized the grace of God in Jesus Christ our Lord, you might have seen the supreme proof of grace in this incarnation of His, whereby he took to Himself man's soul and body.

(Augustine, *The City of God*, x.29)

The Historical Process of Gift and Reception

Our primary task in this chapter is to explicate the New Testament depiction of our basic presupposition that Jesus Christ is grace.[1]

1. The discussion of presuppositions requires some comment on the notions of hermeneutical method or theory that are involved. From the order of these chapters, it should be clear that the presentation of the gospel and its meaning is primary. The discussion of method follows. Method is important not as a pre-determinant of what can be said but as an explication and assessment of what has been said. Methodological questions are not useful as limitations of proclamation but as means of evaluating the assumptions of a presentation and of drawing these assumptions into overt discussion. So also with theory. Prevailing interpretations of theory emphasize detachment and objectivity. Such an account is, of course, heavily weighted in favor of a discarnate intellect seeking to know the world as object. This second order account is often taken to mean what it is to think or to have a theory about something. But the etymology of *theory* is crucial. To trace *theory* to its origins leads to the word *theater*. This fact often comes as a surprise to those schooled in the Enlightenment, and for whom the word *theory* is associated with things "scientific," "rational," "rigorous," or "intellectual." Or, to turn the matter around, the word *theater* is often associated with activities that, compared to either philosophy or science, are decidedly second class intellectually, e.g., "make believe" or "play." But the English word *theory* is of the same family as the Greek, *theatron* or theater. *Theatron* is akin to *thea*, "sight" and to

Because the gospel is historical, the story of actual events in human history, Christian theology begins with the New Testament proclamation of Jesus of Nazareth, who is Christ. The proclamation of which we speak refers to the phenomenon of Jesus interpreted by the believing community. Gift and reception cannot be separated; we have the phenomenon of Jesus only as it is bound together and presented in the New Testament texts. These records do not provide an uninterpreted portrayal of Jesus; rather, the gospels witness to an encounter with the historical Jesus; and this encounter possesses its character only as the interactivity of engagement and response. The originative historical event can be known only as it was and is appropriated and proclaimed to succeeding generations by the New Testament. Hence, the Jesus we can know is the Jesus of New Testament proclamation. We cannot get behind that historical interaction; we can only know Jesus as he is witnessed to by the New Testament authors. These biblical witnesses are multiple, and the presentations they make are multifaceted. The biblical text is inscribed discourse which calls forth further dialogue and ongoing interpretation. The Jesus of New Testament proclamation (kerygma) is the one presented to us for dialogical interaction and continuing interpretation.

The New Testament does not present history and kerymga; rather, it presents what Albert C. Outler calls "kerygmatized history," a his-

---

theasthai, "to view." The verb *theasthai* itself is related to *thauma*, "a thing compelling the gaze" and to *theorein*, meaning "to look at." *Theorein* is the direct antecedent of the Late Latin *theoria*, whence the English *theory*. *Theoria* means "a looking," "a seeing," "an observing," or "a contemplation" and, hence, "a speculation." For an extended discussion, see Poteat, *Walker Percy*, 11–12.

At the heart of the gospel is the saving power of the event that includes the life, death, and resurrection of Jesus, by which, as St. Paul says, God reconciled the world to God's own self. The heart of the gospel is a story—the story of a child born in a time and a place, and of his life, suffering, death, and resurrection. According to this view, the clue and sign of human salvation is found not in science or philosophy but in news of an actual, historical event involving a specific person. The presentation of the gospel is the telling of a story, and theology begins with a recital of that story. Theology also interprets that story, delineating its character and its meaning; theology explores the telling of that story in the New Testament, drawing out its salient features and representing its vitality and truth value. The effort in these considerations of grace is to undertake this theological task.

tory that reflects and evokes life transformation.[2] To separate history and kerygma is distorting because the separation would disjoin what was conceived and expressed holistically.

Operating on the assumption that the New Testament as a whole is the most reliable material we possess for reconstructing a depiction of Jesus, the interpretation we are pursuing is an effort to provide a holistic description of Jesus as proclaimed in the New Testament canon. The final canonical form is constituted by several layers that are a composite of that which is given and interpreted, so that the given interpreted becomes the new given, which is again interpreted. For instance, the Markan source is itself a composite proclamation of Jesus, a composite proclamation that then becomes a given that is inextricably related to other interpretations, such as Matthew or Luke. From the perspective that each of these documents needs to be interpreted within the total canonical structure, our study of the proclaimed Jesus proceeds.

There is movement from the originating historical event/interpretation through successive rounds of interpretation. Consequently, the question may be pressed: why not attempt to determine the earliest materials and make them the privileged material for interpretation? Or, at least, why not stop with pre-redacted materials? But there are no preredacted materials. All of the materials are presented as components of editorial (interpreter) intention. Nevertheless, if the New Testament can be seen as a set of concentric circles, a primary role may still be attributed to the inner circles. For instance, the Synoptic Gospels are more central than the Pastoral Epistles, and Paul is more central than Jude. Even so, there is an advantage in looking at the canon in its totality. Taking all parts into account does not mean that every part has equal weight. To take the canon whole is to take it as a body of materials which has its own character structure as a series of mutually conditioning hermeneutical interplays. In this light, we can explore the

---

2. Taken from Outler, "Shaping the Christological Dogma," in which he clarifies much of the historical development of Christology. We are, in this chapter, concerned with the New Testament witness; a full christological statement would additionally require consideration of dogmatic development in the church, a development which at its best was an effort to respond to "kergymatized history" in freshly creative ways.

canonical proclamation of Jesus and its presentation of God's character and intention as expressed in the New Testament kerygma.

From the beginning in the New Testament text, there is an inseparable connection between what Edward Schillebeeckx calls "the phenomenon of Jesus" and interpretations of this event by disciples.[3] The interinvolvement continues through succeeding generations and with continual buildup. Consequently, succeeding generations take the text and interpret its meaning for a new situation. After the formation of the canon, in every valid continuation in the church, the interpreters stand before the text to allow it to speak as life-shaping authorization in their own situation. This understanding removes the possibility of ever beginning simply "from below" (that is, with the phenomenon of Jesus), or simply "from above" (that is, with a philosophical preunderstanding that controls what the text will be allowed to say). The interactions from below and above cannot be disconnected because the total process conveys the kerygmatic message. This dynamic operates in every reading of the New Testament, including our present depiction of Jesus as grace.

Glory and Grace

In the Old Testament God's glory, *kebod Yahweh*, indicates God's presence, God's "weightiness," among the covenant people. God's glory is the shining radiance of God's presence and activity for human redemption. Furthermore, God's glory is a living, continual self-presenting through God's acts. The two major Old Testament self-revelations of God are the Exodus from Egypt and deliverance from Babylon. Also, the residence of glory in the Temple testified to the concrete reality of both the election of and promise for the Hebrew people. Acknowledgment of God's glory places a demand upon the covenant people, for they are to convey the manifestation of God's glory.[4]

3. See Schillebeeckx, *Jesus*, 51.

4. For a suggestive study of glory and grace, see Hanson, *Grace and Truth*, especially 10–12. Hanson argues that mercy as the lasting and steadfast love of God is fundamental to the New Testament interpretation of the incarnation and best relates the Old Testament themes of *ḥesed* and *emeth* to the New Testament theme. Consequently, this theme of mercy constitutes the best total interpretation of God as revealed in Jesus Christ.

In the New Testament, the glory of God is exhibited in the life, death, and resurrection of Jesus Christ. God "has shone in our hearts to give the light of the knowledge of the glory of God in the face of Jesus Christ" (2 Cor 4:6). In the Fourth Gospel, there is a dual revelation of God's glory before the world (John 2–12) and before the community (John 13–21). In this Gospel, the glory of God is made manifest in Jesus (John 1:14; 13:31; 17:5) as he encounters actual conditions of human life (John 5:39–44; 7:18; 11:4). In Jesus's encounter with destructive human conditions, God's glory is revealed (John 12:27–43).

The glory of God as expressed in Jesus Christ is not a personal possession or located in exemplary qualities of Jesus's life. Rather, the glory of God is the operation of the will of God in this human being. Jesus is the mediator of God's intention, the incarnate expression of God's way of being in relation to human life. Jesus lets God's glory shine through him by carrying out the mission that God has given him. This glory is seen in the totality of Jesus's life, death, and resurrection, with the death and resurrection bringing to greatest clarity God's sovereign presence in Jesus, wherein God's glory is visible to all who believe.

In God's activity in Jesus Christ, the hope of glory is established, a hope that will reach its fullness in the eschaton. What God has done throughout covenant encounters with humankind—that which is made distinctively known in Jesus Christ—will be brought to fulfillment. God's glory revealed in Jesus points forward to the consummation of God's sovereign reign over all creation. The glory of God, revealed at the center of history in Jesus Christ, makes recognizable God's ubiquitous expression through all creation until the end of time.

The Christian gospel is the story of what God has done in Jesus Christ, and it extends to what God is continuously doing and will do throughout creation. In the person of Jesus, the glory of God is historically expressed. As such, the gospel is historical. It conveys a story in human history, a story that reconstitutes human history. The gospels are written to invite an encounter with the proclaimed Jesus. Consequently, theology must explore the originative kerygma and enable its conveyance through critical reconstruction.

Historical Gospel

The heart of the gospel is not a philosophical argument but rather the story of a life lived in a specific time and place: the account of Jesus' life, death, and resurrection. As a story in its telling, the gospel includes the reaction and interpretation of those who witnessed it and who repeat it. The gospel is, therefore, also a confession of meaning found through relationship with this person. The proclaimed Jesus is the one who has come to draw people to himself in such a way that they discover that this relationship is the good news of God for their lives.

Consequently, Christian proclamation is not in its origin a speculative exercise. Rather, Christian proclamation finds its foundation in the concrete story of Jesus and in the response of disciple faith. This story, this kergymatized history, constitutes the point of beginning for Christian theology. Because this story establishes new relationship and a new perspective from which life (both individual life and corporate life) finds vitalizing meaning, it functions as revelation, and salvation lies in indwelling this story.

The importance of the event of Jesus Christ is twofold. First, he conveys the reality of God present for human life: "And the Word became flesh and lived among us, and we have seen his glory, the glory as of a father's only son, full of grace and truth. . . . From his fullness we have all received, grace upon grace" (John 1:14, 16). When we are encountered by Jesus Christ, we are met by God in God's truest mode of being. Grace is God's way of being, a way of being that the incarnation makes definitive as it establishes the possibility of our community with God and with one another. Second, Jesus Christ, as grace, manifests the truest mode of human existence. As gracious establisher and receiver of covenant, Jesus Christ expresses most truly both the divine and human modes of being. God present evokes responsive presence; hence, grace establishes the fundamental paradigm of true Godhood and true humanity.

But in what ways are such affirmations actually grounded in the New Testament proclamation itself? Is there enough unity among the New Testament witnesses to claim that the identity of the proclaimed Jesus is secure? If so, can the identified one be understood as grace?

In the New Testament, we find both unity and diversity, as seen in the divergent emphases of C. H. Dodd and Rudolf Bultmann. Dodd claimed to have found a unified kerygma outlined in the apostolic preaching in the book of Acts. According to Dodd, this outline presents the cohering skeleton for the entire New Testament proclamation. Bultmann, in contrast, insisted upon the diverse emphases of the various New Testament writers and found no way of establishing a coordinated perspective. Although Bultmann, with his emphasis on diversity, won the earlier discussions, the issue is hardly settled. Thus, while James Dunn sees diversity as dominant, he also argues that the definitive expression of Christian faith was in a person, Jesus Christ, so that personal communication is the primary reality. But can we speak of a New Testament unity that coheres around the person of Jesus? Is there diversity within unity or diversity cohering around unity? Dunn argues that there is a common post-Easter kerygma that 1) proclaims Jesus as risen and exalted, 2) calls for faith commitment, and 3) promises a Spirit relationship.[5]

What is distinctive of Christian witness? It is Jesus who is confessed, not an idea, ideology, faith, or teaching, and it is the present status of Jesus that is confessed. Yet, even in this common confession, there is diversity, a diversity most evident in the differences among Christians who are from Palestinian Judaism, Hellenistic Judaism, and Gentile traditions. Nonetheless, as Dunn rightly sees, we can still find a common, unified witness to the healing, teaching Messiah, to the crucified Jesus, and to the resurrected and exalted Lord.

From the first verse of Matthew, where we are introduced to "Jesus Christ," to the last verses of Revelation, where the invocation of Jesus's triumphant reign leads to the intercession that "the grace of the Lord Jesus be with all the saints," the New Testament witness presents this person and his significance as inextricably intertwined. Jesus is presented as possessing a unique filial relation to God. God is supremely active in Jesus, the supreme agent of God's redemptive identification with humankind and with all creation.

---

5. Dunn, *Unity and Diversity*, 30, 56, 58.

Dimensions of Messiahship

The gospel's proclamation of Jesus is rooted in his active life as a healing and teaching messiah. The depiction of his activities and the interpretation of their significance cannot be sundered. The evidence of God present in Jesus was not clear to every observer, and, indeed, there is recognition of the capacity of people to find alternative interpretations for the activity of Jesus: "He is possessed by Beelzebub" (Mark 3:22). But for those whom Jesus encountered and transformed, his life was a manifestation of the glory of God. In his activity and teaching, Jesus was the revealer of God.

Jesus reveals God by creating a relationship with persons, a relationship that establishes a true way of being with God, and being with God makes possible the discovery of truth. Revelation authors new relationship, for revelation and the divine presence are closely interrelated. Life in covenant with God expresses a central reorganization of existence. In Christ, all things are made new.

Revelation and redemption are thoroughly interfaced. To be redeemed is to be in right relationship with God; it is to be in positive community with God and with our neighbors. This understanding of revelation and redemption is social as well as individual, for revelation creates community both with God and with other persons. The interdependence of individual and community means that wholeness is experienced as there is mutual interaction between God and human beings, and as there is interaction among human beings. Both sin and redemption have systemic and individual dimensions. Salvation is the true ordering of life in its multiple relationships, for revelation and redemption point to the authoritative structuring of human life by God. In the authorization of new life by God in Jesus Christ, relationship with God, with people, and with the entire natural order are reoriented.

But the central issue before us is how Jesus Christ exemplifies grace as God with us. Because the gospel is historical, we are obligated to look at particular events; but what is important is not an itemization of these events, but rather, how the historical particulars convey personal presence. That is, the effort is to discern the presence of God enacted in the variety of episodes and reports of Jesus in his historical setting.

Jesus's presence is not that of a God-seeker but that of a seeking God; Jesus represents God as One who does not await human searching. Jesus's seeking cuts across normal social and religious divisions; it is a seeking that risks itself for the possibility of reconciled relationship. Presence, as manifest in Jesus, comes as invitation, with the possibility of acceptance or rejection. Reconciliation in found in acceptance; judgment is found in rejection.

The gospels depict Jesus as one who comes as vulnerable strength. His covenantal invitation, his presence as God's sovereign goodness, demands the just ordering of life and human wholeness; sovereign goodness also stands over against malformation of social and personal life. Accounts of a seeking father (Luke 15:20–24), of a good neighbor (Luke 10:30–37), of the good shepherd (Luke 15:1–7), and of the host for dinner (Luke 14:16–24) all present the theme of grace.

In his person, Jesus embodies the arrival of the kingdom that reveals the glory of God. The reign of God is God's presence exercising judgment and reconciliation in the concrete events of historical existence. Proclamation of this truth, telling the story of Jesus, proclaiming his meaning, is the intention of the New Testament. Acknowledging response to this presentation affirms the authority of Jesus as the claiming center who shapes our existence so as to create distinctive personhood. To be a disciple is to live under the aegis of Jesus, Lord and Redeemer. Indications of the good news of God are found in the proclamation of Jesus as healing, teaching Messiah; but clear recognition of these aspects of Jesus's career are viewed retrospectively from the events of the crucifixion and the resurrection.

There are two foci in the discussion of redemption: God's redeeming activity and human response. Hence, elliptical awareness is required to explore the dynamics of the wholeness of God, a wholeness that makes human life whole.

The New Testament offers differing presentations of the death of Jesus, with contrasting emphases. In Paul's theology of Christ crucified, the wisdom of God seems a foolish contradiction of human wisdom; yet, the strength of God, expressed by the weakness of the cross, is stronger than human capacity. In the book of Acts, the death of Jesus is a negative condition that God sets right in Jesus's resurrection. The twofold event—cross and resurrection—is the foundation of human redemption. In Hebrews, Jesus's death is the act of high priesthood that brings release for a fallen world. In John, Jesus's death reveals the victory of light over darkness. Nonetheless, these various perspectives share a central understanding: God is savingly present to humankind through the cross and resurrection.

By word and action, Jesus proclaimed his controlling conviction of the nearness of God's rule—the sovereignty of grace made plain and brought near. Through word and deed, God's presence is enacted. The character of God's nearness is crucial, for in nearness grace is known. God is near as grace; God is gracious presence.

The understanding of God as grace centers in the death of Jesus. The nearness of God's rule, which determined Jesus's earthly life, was preeminently present in his death. In the cross and resurrection, gracious presence evokes the responsive presence of faith. The question of faith in Jesus was and is the question of faith in God. In the final analysis, faith in Jesus is the point where faith in God is truly and clearly decided.

From the relationlessness of death, new relationship is established.[6] Life and death are brought into new interaction as Jesus's death brings life. In Jesus's death, God participates in the travail of lostness, negation, anguish, and suffering. At both personal and corporate levels, God is immediately involved in the wretchedness of this death. By identifying with human godlessness and guilt, by taking denial of presence upon himself and, in spite of this rejection, creating the relationship of resurrected living, God acts in Jesus's death the activity of grace. Grace expresses God's nature, motive, and way of acting in relation to human life.

As the New Testament centrally testifies, Christian faith is a resurrection faith, for the resurrection event calls faith into being. There are, however, diverse accounts about the specific historical facts surrounding the event. Mark stops with amazed fear; Paul describes resurrection encounters and affirms its necessity for Christian faith; Matthew

---

6. See Jüngel, *Death*, 101.

and Luke emphasize the culminating and inaugurating character of the resurrection; and John weaves the resurrected Jesus into his entire account.

In spite of the variety in these accounts, they share the most important assumption. In the resurrection, Jesus's life and death are vindicated, the disciples experience new life, and God has acted in a decisive way in human history. The resurrection is not produced by the disciples' faith; on the contrary, this event happened to them as the interaction of givenness and reception is tightly woven. Jesus, whom they had known, now meets them in new form and with new power. This Jesus is acknowledged, then proclaimed, as the risen and exalted Lord. This proclamation of God present seeks to evoke faith, and the promise offered in this proclamation is the continuing vitality of Christian life.

In responsive presence, resurrection faith points to a new reality. God present, revealed in the life and death of Jesus, becomes newly creative. Only at Easter does the identity of Jesus as the reigning Christ become clearly manifest. In the resurrection, God is present; grace is known.

The kerygmatic presentation of Jesus's story evokes radical decision about God present. The New Testament witness is not made simply to record history or to convey the writers' own values or evaluations. Rather, the writings are intended to draw those who read or hear the accounts into relationship with Jesus, whom they present. The recital of grace is for the purpose of prompting responsive self-presenting. The purpose is, throughout the New Testament, to write so that those who read may believe, and that believing, they may have life in Jesus Christ (John 20:31). As Charles Wesley puts it:

> Come, let us, who in Christ believe,
> Our common Savior praise;
> To him with joyful voices give
> The glory of his grace.[7]

---

7. See "Hymn 200" in Wesley, *Works* (OUP edition), 7:330–31.

Presence—Divine and Human

We have confidently spoken of the presence of God in the indicative mood. What are the assumptions underlying our claim that God is present?

God is known as present in actual encounter. God present is an affirmation of faith. To assert that God is present is neither to propose a theory of presence nor to present an argument to convince those who do not know that God is actually present.

In the self-presenting of God in Jesus of Nazareth, in this unique, specific, historical person, God present becomes the constitutive fact of Christian existence. For theology, presence is not a problem; it is a presupposition—a gracious presupposition. Presence is not to be found at the conclusion of a debate, but at the commencement of life in Christ.

For Christian theology, understanding the presence of God arises from concrete life in covenant. Interpretation of God present arises from the practice of the presence and is not to be identified with imaginative construction or as the result of abstract contemplation.

God present is known in response to God's self-giving. By offering the divine self in relationship, God calls forth a response of loving gratitude and faithful obedience. To be in Christ is to be aware of God present—and to have one's own presence established.

We sometimes speak of a person as possessing a presence. Such persons create an orbit and carry weightiness. To have a presence is to be self-possessed, to possess a sense of confidence, and to act with assurance. In terms of Christian interpretation, self-possession is not self-creation or a condition achieved by personal intention or strength. Rather, the strength of human presence is created by the presence of God and derives from confidence in God. Jesus is the epitome of possessed presence. He creates his own orbit and conveys a sense of strength that takes initiative in establishing relationships. Jesus's presence graciously creates the possibility of human presence with God, and, consequently, of presence with other persons.

As witnessed to in the New Testament and mediated by word and sacrament, the presence of Jesus is the presence of God. In Protestant traditions, the presence of Jesus is mediated by means of grace: in the words of Scripture as read, heard, and studied; and in preaching, prayer, and Christian community. In the Catholic tradition, the presence of Jesus is celebrated in the sacraments.

Such contemporary media of presence derive from the historical presence of Jesus of Nazareth. And this historical person is known through the narrative given in the New Testament. In this narrative, which is a reconstruction by faith, Jesus is Immanuel and is known through his history. The narrative of Jesus, a narrative embodied in a single life shaped within a specific tradition, moves from birth, through ministry, to death and resurrection. This story is told to make clear the way God was present, is present, and will be present. God is with us in this historical person who has, by encounter, called faith into being. Faith, created by presence, is also responsive presence.

CHAPTER FOUR

Grace and Creation

All things came into being through him.

(John 1:3)

God's Grandeur

The world is charged with the grandeur of God.
  It will flame out, like shining from shook foil;
  It gathers to a greatness, like the ooze of oil
Crushed. Why do men then now not reek his rod?
Generations have trod, have trod, have trod;
  And all is seared with trade; bleared, smeared with toil;
  And wears man's smudge and shares man's smell: the soil
Is bare now, nor can foot feel, being shod.

And for all this nature is never spent;
  There lives the dearest freshness deep down things;
And though the last lights off the black West went
  Oh, morning, at the brown brink eastwards, springs—
Because the Holy Ghost over the bent
  World broods with warm breast and with ah! bright wings.[1]

(Gerard Manley Hopkins)

Creation is an activity of grace. Intimations of grace are present throughout the biblical narrative, but in retrospect from the event of

---

1. Hopkins, "God's Grandeur."

Jesus Christ, this fact is most fully and clearly recognized: "In the beginning was the Word. . . . all things were made by him and without him was not anything made that was made" (John 1:1–3); and "He is the image of the invisible God, the first born of all creation; for in him all things were created" (Col 1:15–16; Heb 1:2). Thus, the proclamation of Jesus Christ sets the New Testament context for thought about creation, thinking that focuses on the "new creation" effected by Jesus Christ and whose interest in the original creation is subordinated to this normative event.[2]

Yet, from the vantage point of Jesus Christ, it is possible and theologically necessary to speak of original creation. From the beginning, Trinitarian emphasis is fundamental to the Christian understanding of God as it ties together the incarnation, the creation, and the Spirit presence. For God present in Jesus Christ is Creator; God the Creator is present in Jesus Christ; and God the Creator and Redeemer is present as Holy Spirit. From the standpoint of the grace made known in Jesus Christ, we have an entry point for interpreting the meaning of creation.

Grace in Creation

To be discovered by God is to discover grace. Grace is the incarnate event that opens our awareness of God and discloses the world to us. In acknowledging God's specific and redeeming presence in Jesus Christ, we are driven to a fundamental implication: creation, all creation, is an expression of grace.

Whereas philosophical theism has often led Christian theology astray by first developing a doctrine of God and then fitting Jesus Christ into the independently developed ideas, our thesis is that the understanding of God is radically and consistently to be developed in the light of Jesus Christ. On the basis of who God is known to be in Jesus Christ, we state our theme: grace is God's way of relating to the world as Creator, Redeemer, and Sustainer.

In Jesus Christ, in originative creative action and in continuing presence, God's gracious being is expressed in every activity of God.

---

2. See Reumann, *Creation*, 20.

Karl Barth makes the point that God's "whole being in all the heights and depths of the Godhead, is simply grace."[3] As Barth presses the point, "Grace is the distinctive mode of God's being in so far as it seeks and creates fellowship by its own free inclination and favour."[4] This "seeking" and "creating" is God's Trinitarian activity. Or to reiterate Hopkins's poetic inspiration,

> The world is charged with the grandeur of God.

God as Creator is the gracious initiator of all reality: "In the beginning God created. . . . And God saw that the light was good" (Gen 1:1, 4). God as Creator is the free agent who calls being out of nothing. Where God, who is alpha, the beginner, and God's will become manifest, creation comes into being and possesses order. The gracious creator does not begrudge the existence of reality apart from God's own self; indeed, God establishes the creation as good.

Having affirmed that God is Creator, the cause of all things, we must step back, look soberly at the phenomenon of the natural world, and enter a caveat. Nature, taken on the whole, is not easy to read and may be understood in contradictory ways. It is not a simple, straightforward, and obvious fact that God's glory or grace is evident in the natural order. Thus Emily Dickinson describes the indecipherable character of nature:

> But nature is a stranger yet;
> The ones that cite her most
> Have never passed her haunted house
> Nor simplified her ghost.
>
> To pit those that know her not
> Is helped by the regret
> That those who know her know her less
> The nearer her they get.[5]

Similarly, in "Wordsworth in the Tropics," Aldous Huxley reflects on Wordsworth's lines from "Tintern Abbey":

---

3. Barth, *Church Dogmatics* II/1, 358.
4. Ibid., 353.
5. Quoted in Daiches, *God and the Poets*, 158–59.

> For I have learned
> To look on nature, . . .
> And I have felt
> A presence that disturbs me with the joy
> Of elevated thoughts; a sense of sublime . . .

Huxley comments:

> In the neighborhood of latitude fifty north, and for the last hundred years or thereabouts, it has been an axiom that Nature is divine and morally uplifting. For good Wordsworthians . . . a walk in the country is the equivalent of going to church, a tour through Westmorland is as good as a pilgrimage to Jerusalem. To commune with the fields and waters, the woodlands and the hills, is to commune, according to our modern and northern ideas, with the visible manifestations of the "Wisdom and Spirit of the Universe."
>
> The Wordsworthian who exports this pantheistic worship of Nature to the tropics is liable to have his religious convictions somewhat rudely disturbed. Nature, under a vertical sun, and nourished by the equatorial rains, is not at all like that chaste, mild deity who presides over the *Gemütlichkeit*, the prettiness, the cosy sublimities of the Lake District. The worst that Wordworth's goddess ever did to him was to make him hear
>
>> Low breathings coming after me, and sounds
>> of undistinguishable motion, steps
>> almost as silent as the turf they trod;
>
> was to make him realize, in the shape of "a huge peak, black and huge," the existence of "unknown modes of being." He seems to have imagined that this was the worst Nature could do. A few weeks in Malaya or Borneo would have undeceived him. Wandering in the hothouse darkness of the jungle, he would not have felt so serenely certain of those "Presences of Nature," those "Souls of Lonely Places," which he was in the habit of worshipping on the shores of Windermere and Rydal. The sparse inhabitants of the equatorial forest are all believers in devils. When one has visited, in even the most superficial manner, the places where they live, it is difficult not to share their faith. The jungle is marvellous, fantastic, beautiful; but it is also terrifying, it is also profoundly sinister. There is

something in what, for lack of a better word, we must call the character of great forests even in those of temperate lands which is foreign, appalling, fundamentally and utterly inimical to intruding man.[6]

Because the separation of grace and nature in Protestant theology was initially axiomatic, the relation between them has remained problematic. John Calvin, for instance, spoke of a "diabolical science . . . which fixes our contemplations on the works of nature and turns them away from God."[7] Calvin further comments: "It would seem as if the more perspicacity men have in observing second causes in nature, they will rest in them more determinedly, instead of ascending by them to God."[8]

Even though the tendency to treat nature as complete in itself remains dominant, the relation of grace and nature has a long historic precedence in Christian thought and a dynamism that must not be lost. Two options are available: clarify the meaning of *nature*, or drop the use of this term and find a substitute such as *creation*, as Claude Y. Stewart has done. Stewart writes:

> Disgraceful ideas lead to disgraceful results. The problematical, limited, modern understanding of nature affects our lives at every turn; and what is more pressing, the environmental crisis results from it. Since nature is a mere thing—machine, resource, stage—we can do with it as we wish; and we proceed to exploit nature to the hilt. Our graceless understanding of nature leads us to treat nature disgracefully. Our question then is this: How can we come to see nature again as the arena of divine glory and grace?[9]

Although earlier times might have been confident in defining the meaning of *nature*, defining nature is no longer a simple task. Here again, Stewart's definition is helpful:

---

6. Ibid., 57–59.
7. Comment on Psalm 29:5 in Calvin, *Commentary on the Book of Psalms*, 479.
8. Comment on Psalm 65:10 in Calvin, *Commentary on the Books of Psalms*, 463. I am indebted to P. Mark Achtemeier for these references.
9. Stewart, *Nature in Grace*, 5.

> Nature, then, as the concept is used today, tends to refer both to "the totality of all powers and processes conceived as a systematic whole" and to that which exists apart from human artifice—to the extra cultural aspect(s) of creation. But in both the wider and the narrower usages, "nature" is marked by complex interrelatedness and by plasticity. It is viewed holistically, a complex, interrelational, novelty producing process; and its various, concretely experienceable aspects (trees, dogs, mountains) are products of this process.[10]

The emphases upon the complex, dynamic, open character of nature move us immediately beyond inherited notions of grace as static or simple. Nature is not to be viewed as self-contained, as a tool for human use, or as only a setting for human history. Rather, nature is the dynamic arena in which God is working, and, therefore, the arena in which God's grace is expressed.

To separate nature and grace is to divide the total work of God and to misperceive both nature and grace. Yet, Protestant theologians often have made such a separation. What we are striving for is an understanding that is inclusive and integrative of the activity of the triune God, but one that sees grace and nature, as Stewart argues, in creative interaction.

One clear advantage of speaking of "grace and creation" rather than "grace and nature," is that "creation" does not possess a history of being understood as self-contained and self-sustaining. On the contrary, the implication of creation is a Creator; interdependency is thus implied from the outset.

Our understanding of creation reflects our interpretation of God's arena of operation and the character of God's activity in that arena. To put this another way, the understanding of God's grace in Jesus Christ and God's gracious expression in all creation are coordinates. The incarnation refers to the relation of God to the totality of the created order, both to human history and to natural history.

More particularly, God's free action in the specific historical event of Jesus Christ interprets God's free action in all creation. Hence, when we assert that God's intentional action comes to definitive expression

10. Ibid., 285.

in Jesus Christ, we also insist that the cosmic creation is related to that event and that that event makes evident God's grace in the totality of creation.

Two assumptions are basic in these statements. First, we are building upon an understanding of God as freely acting in the incarnation and, therefore, in all relationships to the created order. Second, we are building upon an understanding of creation as an arena for the expression of grace.

The first assumption has been present throughout our consideration of grace. God's intentional activity of self-disclosure in Jesus Christ is the supreme act by which grace is understood and by which any activity of grace may be recognized. God is the intentional agent who is freely self-revealing in Jesus Christ. God, as freely acting through self-giving, is expressed not only in the dynamic structure of history but also in nature. The total arena is the field of divine activity, and divine activity in every expression intends relationship.

This perspective of creation is analogous to an interpretation of creation in the Old Testament from the perspective of the exodus/covenant event.[11] The historical priority of the establishment of the covenant to the written interpretations of the creation provides an order of knowledge: God's creation of covenant extends to the creation of all things. Themes of God's initiative, God's affirmation of the creation as good, God's faithfulness, even to a disordered or falsely ordered creation, God's renewal of the divine intention for creation, and God's ultimate purposes for creation are all themes which are extrapolated from the exodus/covenant event.

Likewise, all autobiography and biography, whether of communities or individuals, functions by this principle: In the light of the most significant events, one interprets one's past and projects one's future. Because the exodus/covenant was the critical event in Israelite self-understanding, from that event a perspective is given on the rest of life. From the vantage point of this most significant event, God's activity as creator is interpreted.

---

11. John Reumann's claim that there are multiple ways to develop an Old Testament understanding of creation is cited by Philip J. Hefner, "The Creation," in Braaten and Jenson, *Christian Dogmatics*, 1:275.

The doctrine of creation is not so much an explanation as it is an affirmation. In the New Testament, this affirmation is an expression of gratitude: God present in Jesus Christ is the same God present from the beginning who will be present until the end. This presence, as known in Jesus Christ, is an expression of redemptive love. The doctrine of creation is not an effort to give a Christian twist to a philosophically or scientifically established point of beginning (if such a point could be established). Rather, the doctrine of creation is a theological song of praise. It is an interpretation of the totality of life under the aegis of God's redemptive presence. All creation is rooted in God's good pleasure, is sustained by God's enduring favor, and finds its goal in God's providential will.

John Wesley's hymn indicates the understanding of creation which Jesus Christ effects:

> How beauteous nature now!
> How dark and sad before!
> With joy we view the pleasing change,
> and nature's God adore.[12]

The assumption of the goodness of creation is the assumption of positive relationship. Because goodness is the original intention of God's creation, injustice, destruction of the earth and of the natural order, as well as the destruction or dispiriting of human life, are abnormal and distorting malformations. Because God is present to the creation, conditions are ripe for responsive acknowledgement. From the new creation given in Jesus Christ, Christian interpretation is open to God's activity in original creation. The same God present in Jesus Christ is present in the beginning—the God of grace. Creation originates in the good grace of God. God's goodness is inherently relational and endows the creation with goodness as it stands in relation to God.

The grace of God underwrites the ongoingness of the created order so that there is providential guidance and ultimate hope. Because God is omega, the end of all things, the doctrine of creation is an eschatological affirmation. The persistent presence of God's sustaining grace continues what God expresses in redemptive renewal and origi-

---

12. "We Lift Our Hearts to Thee," in Wesley, *Collection of Psalms and Hymns*, 65.

nal creation. In each activity the same divine intention and character is expressed. Creation is not yet complete; there is continuous struggle against all forces that destroy good and deny grace.

Consequently, God as divine agent acts in and through history and nature as the presence of God is expressed in the concreteness of actual events. Even as a human agent is not "alongside" his or her bodily actions, so God is present in nature and history and acts through concrete events. Yet God possesses dimensionalities not subsumable under nature and history, not exhausted by the totality of nature and history.

If it is allowed that grace might be expressed in the natural and historical order, can we indicate either general or special cases where this is so? Can we, from the vantage point of God's revelation in Jesus Christ, discover the gracious working of God in natural and historical processes? We make the bold claim that the processes supporting the total organic structure, the emergence of the variety of life forms, the stewardship of life by life, and the emergence of reciprocal intentionality in human beings are such evidence. In these processes gracious presence is known, and through these processes grace is operative.

There is a continuum through all creation. While clear distinctions can be drawn between sections of this continuum, so that geological history may be distinguished from human historical events, there is also permeative connectedness, so that change in any part of the continuum is reflected through and can be felt in the whole continuum. Both differentiation and connection are to be recognized, and each may, under particular circumstances, be emphasized. Nonetheless, there is an interrelatedness rooted in God's originating creation, in the particularity and consistency of God's way of being in relation to creation, and in God's ultimate intention for all creation.

We are not searching for natural laws or structural patterns that would designate the sinews of grace, for grace is a person and operates through personal agency. God continuously relates to creation by calling it into being through ubiquitous presence, through granting contingent rationality, and through renewing encounter. The entire created order is recipient of God's presence and is subject to God's encounter.

There are indications in the Bible that all creation is affected by the human fall and needs re-creation (Gen 3:14–19; Isa 24:4–6; 24:17–20; Rev 21–22). Since alienation from God is a decisional matter, it is possible to argue that the inadequate or corrupt stewardship by fallen human beings can affect the natural world, as our ecological crisis makes frighteningly evident. The entire creation bears the bruises and destruction caused by the exploitative aggressiveness of human sin.

Yet once again, God is faithful, and that which is created by grace is sustained by grace. God's continuous creativity struggles with the actual abuses of nature by humankind. There is no assurance that human beings will not bring about the destruction of the earth. The planet on which we live is finite and temporal; it has an end, but it may be destructively brought to its end—it may go out with a blast or a sigh. Yet, because God prevails as Redeemer and Sustainer, "because the Holy Ghost over the bent / World broods with warm breast and with ah! bright wings," the renewal of creation is possible.[13]

Creation is never, from a Christian perspective, viewed as independent from God. There are no self-derived and self-maintained creative or sustaining energies. In Jesus Christ, we see God and the world together. The Christian vision is a holism of interaction in which God and the world are graciously related.

Creation Out of Nothing and Continuing Creation

Because the confession that God is Creator is an affirmation made from the perspective of God's re-creation in Jesus Christ and through the Holy Spirit, the confession of God as Creator is a confession of the Trinity. The original creation is known to be God's creation because it is so perceived from the vantage point of the incarnation. God present in Jesus Christ and as Holy Spirit makes possible the recognition of God present in creation; God present in the specific person of Jesus Christ and through the direct engagement by the Holy Spirit opens the way to recognizing God present in all things. Specific presence opens the way to recognition of ubiquitous presence. Hence, in the

---

13. Hopkins, "God's Grandeur," lines 13–14.

order of knowing, to be re-created by God through covenantal relationship is to be given the perspective from which all creation is to be understood.

Creation out of nothing (*creatio ex nihilo*) is witness to the divine freedom expressed in the free grace of creation. Creation is the gratuitous expression of God's love, an unnecessitated act of agape that expresses the Creator's nature. The creation is good because, given by God in freedom, it expresses God's love.

Continuous creation (*creatio continua*) emphasizes God's continuous creative presence in every present moment of existence. Creation is not only originally dependent upon God but is also at every moment dependent upon God's gracious presence. The interactive, ongoing relationship of God and creation is a precondition of having being.

Grace and Created Goodness

Creation in grace establishes the reality of relationship. As Thomas Aquinas puts it, "creation in the creature is only a certain relation to the Creator as to the principle of its being."[14] Creation is a gracious communication; it involves a giving and an acceptance of being. This same point is emphasized by Paul Tillich: "Creation through the Word . . . points symbolically both to the freedom of creation and to the freedom of the created."[15] Creation is God's free action, and to understand creation, the first emphasis must be upon the total dependence of all creation upon God. A second emphasis is that, in freedom, God establishes the freedom or integrity of the creature.

The incarnation makes clear the ultimate seriousness with which God grants integrity to creation. The good God creates and calls the creation good: good, that is, in the sense that God's creation possesses potential for positive relationship with God.

Because we speak of nature as fallen, the goodness of the natural order, i.e., of creation, becomes problematic. The tension between positive and negative characteristics of nature is not directly faced by most recent theologians. Even those who speak of the need to include

---

14. Aquinas, *Summa Theologica*, Ia.45.3.
15. Tillich, *Systematic Theology*, 1:158.

the natural world in a discussion of God as Creator tend to turn rapidly to the goodness and fallenness of creation as these qualities pertain to human beings.

This approach—the backbone of late nineteenth- and early twentieth-century idealistic interpretation—was reinforced by Paul Tillich, who began with the premise that since human creatures stand at the apex of creation, human existence provides the metaphysical key for interpreting all reality. Thus Tillich contends:

> Man occupies a pre-eminent position in ontology, not as an outstanding object among other objects, but as that being who asks the ontological question and in whose self-awareness the ontological answer can be found. . . . [man] is able to answer the ontological question himself because he experiences directly and immediately the structure of being and its elements.[16]

Tillich's assumption has not retained convincing power for philosophers and theologians. From one direction, there are those who doubt the foundationalist assumptions of a priori structures as opposed to more historical interpretations of structures of meaning. From another perspective, there are those who reject the radical anthropomorphism of this beginning point, and who would place human beings within nature rather than subordinate nature to human structures.

Moving in a different direction, Karl Barth interprets creation from the perspective of God's act in Jesus Christ. In one sense, Barth continues to utilize a point of reference that is human and historical, but he does so in terms of the character of God expressed in the person of Jesus Christ. Hence, in Christ, God is manifest as gracious Redeemer and, by extrapolation, as gracious creator. The natural world, including human beings, is the free expression of God's grace.

Pursuing this question of the nature of the goodness of God's creation, H. Richard Niebuhr claims:

> whatever is, is good, because it exists as one thing among the many—which all have their origin and their being in the

---

16. Ibid., 60.

> One—the principle of being which is also the principle of value.[17]

and

> Believing man does not say first, "I believe in a creative principle," and then, "I believe that the principle is gracious, that it is good toward what issues from it." He rather says, "I believe in God the Father Almighty Maker of heaven and earth." This is the primary statement, a point of departure and not a deduction. In it the principle of being is identified with the principle of value and the principle of value with the principle of being.[18]

The affirmation of the good Creator underlies the affirmation of the good creation. On the negative side, the theme of the goodness of creation stands in opposition to the idea that the natural world is hostile to or is separated from God. On the positive side, the created order is the sphere of God's presence; it shares in God's glory. But what is the concrete character of goodness as this is ascribed to creation?

Jürgen Moltmann has emphasized both the dynamic and the eschatological characteristics of the created order through its future orientation. The dynamic character of the natural order rules out any static interpretation of the goodness of the natural world as a primordial given or as an achieved state. Goodness, as the character of the Creator, states the intention of the Creator for the creation, but it points to eschatological possibility rather than to past or present actuality. Beginning with creation out of nothing, Moltmann stresses the radical contingency of the world, for what is out of nothing may again become nothing. Therefore, creation is open—open to destruction, continuance, or new creation. With creation, a process is inaugurated: "The field of destructive and constructive possibilities is laid out."[19] The goodness of creation is in its possibility established by God, who, through suffering-identification with the world, brings hope. This identification is found preeminently in Jesus Christ in whom God

---

17. Niebuhr, *Radical Monotheism*, 32.
18. Ibid., 32–33.
19. Moltmann, *Religion*, 36.

participates in the suffering of the world, so as to create a new relationship with all creation.[20]

The good creation, then, is a possibility within the dynamism of the created order. It is a contingent possibility, since the annulment of meaning through destructive denial of being stands as an alternative. Goodness is a possibility as God works to bring the total creation to purpose and meaning. In this sense, the cosmos possesses many potential stories in relation to its Creator—stories of possibility, abuse, death, and rebirth.

In relation to the natural order, the gracious character of God does not necessitate God's creating the best of all worlds, i.e., a world without conflict, evil, or destructive force.[21] Rather, God intends a cre-

---

20. Moltmann, *Crucified God*, 271–75.

21. Adams, *Virtue of Faith*, 56–57, has argued for an understanding of God as Creator which does not imply that an omnipotent, omniscient being must create the best of all possible worlds. Although Adams directly addresses the question of the relation of creation to human beings, the same argument can be made in regard to nature as a whole. As Adams puts it:

> Plato is one of those who held that a perfectly good creator would make the very best world he could. He thought if the creator chose to make a world less good than he could have made, that could be understood only in terms of some defect in the creator's character. Envy is the defect that Plato suggests. It may be thought that the creation of a world inferior to the best that he could make would manifest a defect in the creator's character even if no one were thereby wronged or treated unkindly. For the perfectly good moral agent must not only be kind and refrain from violating the rights of others, but must have other virtues. For instance, he must be noble, generous, high minded, and free from envy. He must satisfy the moral ideal.
>
> There are differences of opinion, however, about what is to be included in the moral ideal. One important element in the Judeo-Christian moral ideal is grace. For present purposes, grace may be defined as a disposition to love which is not dependent on the merit of the person loved. The gracious person loves without worrying about whether the person he loves is worthy of his love. Or perhaps it would be better to say that the gracious person sees what is valuable in the person he loves, and does not worry about whether it is more or less valuable than what could be found in someone else he might have loved. In the Judeo Christian tradition it is typically believed that grace is a virtue which God does have and men ought to have.
>
> A God who is gracious with respect to creating might well choose to create and love less excellent creatures than he could have chosen. This is not to suggest that grace in creation consists in a preference for imperfection

ation that possesses integrity and that has intrinsic value. It is a world that functions with myriads of subordinate ends as well as in terms of its value as a whole. And it is a world to which God continuously relates, always respecting the world's integrity. Divine grace is creative and continuing; it originates and sustains relationship.

Convictions about grace in creation, about possibility for the created order, and about hope in an eschatological good are all rooted in God's self-presentation in Jesus Christ. God's presence within the natural world reveals the divine intention and way of being in and for the world.

The incarnation says a great deal about the world as well as about God. It defines God's way of being as grace and announces the intrinsic integrity and value of the created order. The incarnation is not only enfleshment in human form; it is God's coming in space and time, God's participation in and being purposefully bodied forth for all creation.

---

as such. God could have chosen to create the best of all possible creatures, and still have been gracious in choosing them. God's graciousness in creation does not imply that the creatures he has chosen to create must be less excellent than the best possible. It implies, rather, that even if they are the best possible creatures, that is not the ground for his choosing them. And it implies that there is nothing in God's nature or character which would require him to act on the principle of choosing the best possible creatures to be the object of his creative powers.

Grace, as I have described it, is not part of everyone's moral ideal. For instance, it was not part of Plato's moral ideal. The thought that it may be the expression of a virtue, rather than a defect of character, in a creator, not to act on the principle of creating the best creatures he possibly could, is quite foreign to Plato's ethical viewpoint. But I believe that thought is not at all foreign to a Judeo-Christian ethical viewpoint.

God as gracious changes the considerations, for grace carries a new ground and quality of relationship. As Adams contends, grace is not an excuse for imperfection; rather, it provides the base for understanding the divine Creator in the Judeo-Christian tradition. And that grace is definitively understood as revealed in Jesus Christ.

Nonetheless, Adams's argument is open to debate. It is built on the premise that the argument for the best of all possible worlds is utilitarian. The argument questions the creatures' rights for a perfectly ordered life or the belief that happiness—as self-gratification or self-fulfilling—is an appropriate telos of life. When grace is understood as relationship, the meaning of creation and the goodness of creation are understood as relationship of the Creator with creation; hence, grace establishes the meaning of human existence. Swinburne has endorsed this argument in *Coherence of Theism*, 148, n. 17.

In the incarnation, the Creator honors the creation by coming into its context on its terms and thereby establishes a relationship of mutual respect and recognition of worth. In the incarnation, God honors the world by coming into its malformed context and establishing a relationship that offers redemptive love.

Once again, we are face-to-face with the contingent character of the created order. T. F. Torrance links the incarnation to the world's contingency and intelligibility:

> The interrelation between the incarnation of the Logos and the creation of all things visible and invisible out of nothing by that same Logos, called for a profound rethinking of the relation between God and the world as one in which it is recognized that the radical distinction between uncreated and created being, between the uncreated rationality of God and the created rationality of the world, far from reducing the being and rationality of the contingent world to unreality and insignificance, establishes their reality and secures their significance, not in spite of, but precisely in their contingent character. That is to say, the incarnation has the constant effect of affirming the contingent intelligibility of the creation, reinforcing the requirement to accept it as the specific kind of rationality proper to the physical world, and as the only kind capable of providing evidential grounds for knowledge of the universe in its own natural processes.
>
> The constitutive relation between God and the world which all this implies may be described as neither necessary nor arbitrary, but as both free and rational. The world needs God to be what it is, but God does not need the world to be what he is, the eternally self-existent God who is not dependent on anything other than himself. There is thus an asymmetrical relation between God and the world, characterized by perfect freedom on God's part and sheer dependence on the world's part. Since the Creator was free not to create, his act of creation is to be understood as an act of pure liberality and grace, i.e., a contingent act unconditioned by any necessity in God. It is because the created world is not necessary for God's being but is freely given by him a reality of its own distinct from his,

that it is contingent, independent of any necessity in God but dependent upon the act of his beneficent will.[22]

The contingency yet rationality of the created order for Christian theology points to a transcendent Creator who in freedom and out of grace creates a cosmos out of nothing, yet a cosmos that possesses its own rationality and integrity. Empirical science depends upon the contingency of the created order. (Otherwise, a priori mathematical deduction could be utilized to express inexorable laws of natural necessity.) Empirical science is possible because the world is contingent.[23]

The contingency of the world means that the creation is continuously dependent upon God's creative grace. The multivariable character of nature means that empirical science is always capable of surprising the investigator with its unexpected richness and its own rationality. The openness of contingent nature points toward expanding boundaries of understanding.[24]

---

22. Torrance, *Divine and Contingent Order*, 33–34.

23. See ibid., 17–18, 26, 34–35, 44, 48, and 54.

24. Ibid., 40. Theologians, for centuries, have spoken with confidence about God as Creator. Challenges to particular arguments for the existence of God and for the divine role in creation (e.g., Kant and Hume) have been recognized as difficulties and as leaving the issue undecided but not necessarily as decisive proof against the notion of a creator. (Arguments against divine creation have continued to the present. See, for example, Dawkins, *Blind Watchmaker*. Similarly, Stephen W. Hawking, the preeminent scientist in the fields of general relativity and early cosmology, has described a self-contained universe that has no edge or boundary: "The universe would not be created, not be destroyed; it would simply be." So he asks, "What place, then, for a Creator?" (*Time*, February 8, 1988, 60).

Process theology, which has had notorious trouble with the notion of God as Creator, possesses potential for responding to this mode of thought. See Cobb, *Christian Natural Theology* and Neville, *God the Creator*. But most Christian theology has to come to terms with the radical implications of a scientific view that excludes creation.

The contingency of the world is pivotal. In its contingency, the world is released for empirical investigation and intramundane explanation—complete as it may be, which never totally eliminates the mystery of new surprise. A transcendent Creator remains a possibility for Christian theological interpretation and is not undercut even by increasingly totalistic interpretations of models of the cosmos. The transcendence of God remains, as does the contingency of the created order. The rationality of the created order may be complete in itself and still not bear upon the utterly transcendent Creator God.

If science is concerned with the contingency away from God, theology is concerned with the contingency of the world toward God.[25] Here grace takes center stage as God continuously creates the world, regulates it, and provides it with its inner coherence. Hence, grace represents the dependence and independence of the world in relation to God. In dependence, the world is referred back to its transcendent Creator; in independence, the world possesses its own contingent but inherent freedom. The natural order, including human beings, is continuously receiving God's grace.

Tillich suggests a spanning of the total work of creation as he writes of "originating creation, sustaining creation, and directing creation." This expanded understanding of creation means that not only the preservation of the world but also providence is subsumed under the doctrine of the divine creativity.[26] This span is the reach of the incarnation. It moves from an emphasis on creation out of nothing, to an emphasis on preservation as continuous creation, (which guarantees the continuity of rational structure), to an emphasis on providence and eschatology, as God creatively utilizes the spontaneity and structured wholeness of all creation.[27] This perspective is gained as we discover that in the gracious Creator we live and move and have our being.*

[EDITOR'S NOTE: The author had intended two interrelated sections to complete this chapter. The first was to be "An Ecological Gospel" and the second "An Eschatological Gospel."]

---

25. Torrance, *Divine and Contingent Order*, 60.
26. Tillich, *Systematic Theology*, 253.
27. Ibid., 253–64.

CHAPTER FIVE

Grace upon Grace

He is the image of the invisible God, the first born of all creation; for in him all things were created, in heaven and on earth, visible and invisible, whether thrones or dominions or principalities or authorities— all things were created through him and for him. He is before all things, and in him all things hold together. He is the head of the body, the church, he is the beginning, the first born from the dead, that in everything he might be preeminent. For in him all the fullness of God was pleased to dwell, and through him to reconcile to himself all things, whether on earth or in heaven, making peace by the blood of his cross.
(Colossians 1:15–20, RSV)

*Come then, and to my soul reveal
The heights and depths of grace.*[1]

(Charles Wesley)

The nature of grace as revealed in the life, death, and resurrection of Jesus Christ makes possible the recognition of grace in other arenas of life. When we look to Jesus Christ, from this vantage point we discover

---

1. Wesley, Hymn 124 in *Works*, 7:234–36. The hymn is titled "With glorious clouds encompassing round."

previous, pervasive, and promissory workings of grace in human life and in the entirety of creation.

To recognize grace in its most complete and clearest embodiment in Jesus Christ prepares one to recognize God's ubiquitous expressions of grace. God is present everywhere. The heightened sensitivity and the prepared awareness that is effected by God's particular historical relating to humankind makes possible the widest recognition of God's action throughout human history. Consequently, sharp focus on what grace means as manifested in Jesus Christ leads not to rejection of extra-Jesus activity of God; rather, it leads to inclusive recognition and generous affirmation of the manifestations of grace which have been made evident from the vantage point of Jesus Christ.[2] Once acknowl-

---

2. The spectrum of Christian interpretation of interreligious relationships is broad and the disagreements deep. It may be of value to attempt a quick placement of my position among some of the possibilities. I hold to the uniqueness and normativity of Jesus Christ. I do not hold to the exclusivity of Jesus Christ as the only presence of God in the world. Jesus Christ is the definitive statement of who God is. In this sense, he is the way, the singular way from God to humankind. Yet the grace of God is also expressed to others outside of Christ, but this grace also stems from the normative position of Jesus Christ. In this sense, Jesus Christ is the definitive way from God to human beings and from human beings to God.

I find the Frankfurt Declaration (1970) and the Lausanne statements (1974), both evangelical affirmations, overly restrictive in their exclusive view of Jesus's mediatorship. Nonetheless, the centrality of Christ and the authority of Scripture I do find congenial, and my position represents an effort to maintain these emphases.

From Karl Barth I have learned as clearly as from anyone that Jesus Christ is grace; however, I develop this somewhat differently even as I accept his christocentric relativization of all religions. At the same time, I differentiate myself from the development of themes of general revelation by Protestant theologians who have moved to more impersonal grounds that possess tendencies toward historicism. Emil Brunner, Paul Althaus, Paul Tillich, Wolfhart Pannenberg, and Carl Braaten have all developed this more general theme. The chief disagreement I have with these thinkers is that special revelation is viewed from the perspective of general revelation. I would reverse the process completely. General revelation is authentically known as revelation retrospectively, that is, only from the perspective of God's revelation in Jesus Christ. The way is from Jesus Christ outward. "General Revelation" stands for the innumerable ways God has been personally present to people, of the ways God has historically and concretely encountered other people. Such general revelation is to be known and its meaning is to be judged by the revelation in Jesus Christ.

I find some recent Roman Catholic positions suggestive that stress the many ways to God, yet assert that there is one norm. I agree with the emphasis of Karl Rahner, Peter Fransen, and Gregory Baum that grace is always God's personal presence.

edging grace in Jesus Christ, we are prepared to recognize refractions of God's grace where present in the variety of religious traditions.³

Grace and Religious Life

In acknowledging Jesus Christ as God's definitive way of being in the world, Christianity affirms that Jesus Christ is both the judge and fulfiller of every expression or perception of God's character in any religious form. The truth Christianity claims to believe is not found in its own singular possession but is embodied in the Lord to whom Christian faith bears witness. Consequently, it is always inappropriate to compare Christianity to other religions so as to see which expression of worship or ethics is superior and thereby establish the greater value of one religion over another. Rather, the acknowledgement of Jesus as Lord places Christianity under the same normative principles

---

Walbert Buhlmann and Hans Küng carry further Rahner's argument of the salvific value of other religions. Rahner's notion of "anonymous Christians" probably retains a too-triumphalist overtone and tends to move from the many to the one rather than from the one to the many. I do not find it convincing to separate Christ from Jesus or to make the unique historical character of Jesus illustrative of a universal (and prior) principle, as does Paul F. Knitter.

Perhaps most crucial is the ancient theological issue: Does the historical Jesus constitutively effect salvation or is the historical person of Jesus one instance of a universal principle? The dialectic within the Trinity affords our most significant answer. The interaction of holiness and grace, both present in the Godhead, represents an internal struggle in which the historical person of Jesus is thoroughly and necessarily engaged. This engagement reveals what grace is: God's way of being that is manifest actually and definitely in Jesus Christ. Jesus Christ reveals who God is and what God's nature is. The God revealed in Jesus Christ is graciously present to other people through other traditions. This we know from the vantage point of God's specific, historical, constitutive act in Jesus Christ.

3. Karl Barth has rejected religion as human pride, as a means of domesticating God that is unable to distinguish itself from worldly values. One must admit that the history of religions proves that all of these perversions occur. But religious conviction and practice may also convey awareness of God's presence and authentic, even though imperfect and distorted, response to God. Barth's exegesis of Romans is not convincing on this point (see, for instance, Davies, "Dr. Karl Barth's Interpretation of Romans 1, 2," in *Paul and Rabbinic Judaism*, 325–28. The warning Barth issues is valuable as a demand for religious self-criticism; but as a principle, it fails to distinguish the normative presence of God in Jesus Christ from the exclusive presence of God in Jesus Christ. Normativity is the essential point; exclusivity is not to be maintained.

of judgment and fulfillment as any other religion. The significance of Christianity is not found in itself but in that ultimate One to whom it refers all things, including itself.

Humility is required in Christian self-awareness. In pointing to its sovereign Lord, Christian religious life recognizes the norm by which it, along with other religious expressions, is both judged and affirmed: The finality of which Christian faith speaks is the finality of Jesus Christ, not its own character, faith, or merit. There is no room for self-aggrandizement, pride of possession, or preferential status. The good news that Christian faith proclaims is not its own existence in the world or the values it embodies. Rather, Christian faith witnesses to the gracious, reigning Lord who comes with forgiveness and moral claim on all people.

Insofar as being a Christian carries the positive reality of being "in Christ," of participating in the body of Christ, and of finding one's life in the community of those who are in community with Jesus Christ, there is a distinctiveness about Christian existence. But this distinctiveness makes no claim for oneself. To be "in Christ" is to yield all of life to God's glory. To be "in Christ" is to witness by word and life to the singular grace of God, who is our Creator, sustainer, and ultimate hope. The sovereignty of Christ is primary.

The unfolding interactions of givenness and response that we have noted in the New Testament canon continue throughout church history. As a result, the event of Jesus Christ comes to contemporary Christians as an already interpreted event and presents itself in contexts that will require further interpretation of the event.

Thus, transmission is a complicated process. When the kerygmatic Jesus is represented in the present, this presentation carries coloration of the understanding of the kerygma through centuries of the Christian tradition. The kerygma comes to us as theologically reflected upon over a long span of time. As we hear the proclamation, several trajectories come into conjunction: the New Testament proclamation, the historical interpretation (with various weightings by various traditions), and present historical particularities. These historical complexities cannot be easily unraveled.

There is a break, however, between the New Testament proclamation and the succeeding interpretations. The canonical message has a primacy and normativity that no subsequent interpretation possesses. Scripture is more basic than tradition, both as the fountainhead of Christian traditions and as the continuing normative standard by which these traditions are evaluated.

To speak of the authorizing potency of the lordship of Jesus Christ is not to reject all conditioning factors; rather, it is to move into complex interaction with contextual realities, whether internal to Christianity or in the relations of Christian faith to non-Christian faiths. Authority functions in a dialectical manner in that there is imposing claim and receptive response. Our understanding of the authority of Jesus Christ takes the initiative and makes primary claims. These claims are then responded to from within specific historical situations. In the interaction of claim and response to God present, the authority of Jesus Christ utilizes, criticizes, and transforms the actual conditions and shapings of human existence.

Authority is only expressed through particular historical events. Hence, the particularity of Jesus Christ and the particularity of response to him constitute the crux of the claim of Christian authority. As response is made and authority is internalized, life is shaped by the authorizing power. The resulting shape of life is conformity to Christ. The witness made, the message carried, and the spirit of interaction with others is set, even if it is only and always partially achieved. The authority of Christ does not give authority over others but directs us to self-giving to others. Christ as authorizing Lord does not create superiors, but friends who are servants of all humankind (John 13:12–16; 15:12–17).

The Christian Attitude Toward Other Religions

It is impossible to state abstractly what the multiple relations of specific Christian communities will be with other specific religious communities; one can only imagine a great variety of ways of relating among communities of Christians and Muslims, Christians and Buddhists, or Christians and Hindus, for instance. In principle, however, such engagements offer fresh opportunity for discovery, disagreement, affirmation, and distinction. What must be honored is the integrity of each. But what must also be honored is the norm by which Christianity and other religious traditions are judged, both positively and negatively. Jesus as Lord is authoritative precisely as he functions as the authorizing center of life, a center which possesses both centripetal and centrifugal power.

Grace, wherever it makes itself known and is discovered, is known by its comparability to the norm of Jesus Christ; that is, grace in any religious tradition is God's historical engagement to which that tradition bears witness. In acknowledging the broader character and manifestations of grace, we must not conceive of grace as a power, an ambience, an aspect, or dimension of nature. Rather, grace is God, God present through relationship to people and communities, including to the varied religious traditions. The same God expresses the same divine nature in every encounter, although this divine expression may be unrecognized, distorted, denied, or rejected. Grace in Jesus Christ makes Christians sensitively aware of expressions of that same grace in other religions. Where this divine/human relationship is found, the kinship of Christian faith and non-Christian traditions is joyfully affirmed.

Persistently, there has been a temptation to affirm the superiority of Christianity over other religions. This attitude is neither conveyed nor condoned by the gospel. There can be no debating over who is first; to do so is not to understand by what Spirit we live. Christianity should not be self-claiming; it points away from itself to its Lord. All ecclesiastical self-interest must surrender to self-giving. The lordship of Jesus presides over every religious tradition, including Christianity and especially Christianity. Those who know the truth are responsible to it not as its masters but rather as its servants. The central Christian claim of grace calls us to humility, especially in our relations with non-Christians.

The gracious initiative of God is the primary reality. But human response from within a particular religious tradition is also essential to the completion of the hermeneutical circle. Consequently, critical self-awareness about our religious location is necessary. For those in the Christian tradition it is a matter of cardinal importance to recognize that the interactions of religious traditions functions in mutually conditioning ways. As religious traditions encounter one another in our shrinking world, the first point to be made is that traditions are ongoing processes; consequently, they do not encounter one another as fixed entities. The traditioning processes, unfolding in multiple ways, make for a variety of specific intersections and interactions.[4]

Biblical scholarship, for instance, has explored the Old and New Testaments both in response to their environments and against their environments. Both of these emphases are true of every religious tradition. There are appropriations and rejections of contextual realities, including other religious traditions.

Christian Faith, the Old Testament, and Jews

The first and closest relation of Christian faith to another religious tradition is its relation to the Old Testament.[5] The relation of the

---

4. For suggestive comments on this issue see Jennings, "Tradition," 1–2. Hick, *God Has Many Names*, presents options for dialogue among religions. Hick seeks to establish a philosophy of religious pluralism that gives to every religion its own integrity and calls all religions to acknowledge and be open to the integrity of every religious persuasion. Nevertheless, there are indications that some religious traditions "mediate God to mankind better than others" (*God Has Many Names*, 115); and, one might add, this also seems to be the case in a single religious tradition. In Hick's view, adequacy is to be judged through continued truth-seeking dialogue, characterized by the fervent desire to learn from one another.

Hick proposes that if the man Jesus can be separated from the Christian interpretation of him formed over the centuries, there might be fruitful results (123). Since we find this proposal impossible to do on historical and hermeneutical grounds, our own position would fall under Hick's malediction. But Hick's approach is unpromising in itself. With his uncritical assumption of the value-free nature of human reason, and with his separation of the kerygma and tradition, Hick offers no good road into the future.

5. My colleague Robert T. Osborn, in a provocatively insightful article, "Christian Blasphemy," has argued the necessity of Christians recognizing the Jewishness of Jesus and the continuing role of Judaism itself in God's salvation history. Jewish self-understanding includes the conviction that Jews are exclusive instruments of God's universal salvation (340). He rejects Rosemary Radford Ruether's attempt to remove the claim of exclusivity as denaturing Judaism (340–41). Christianity must be pro-Jewish; to this end it is necessary to recognize that the truth of Jesus Christ cannot be separated from the concrete, historical person Jesus (343). And this Jesus is a Jew, "the

Old Testament to the New Testament is interdependent. Jesus cannot be properly understood without knowledge of his prehistory in the Old Testament, for the Old Testament was the Scripture of the early Christian communities as they witnessed to their faith that Jesus was the Messiah. Nor, from a Christian point of view, can the Old Testament be understood without knowledge of the proclaimed Jesus who judges and fulfills the Old Testament. The mutual interplay of these two poles creates canonical unity. The Old Testament is the necessary background for understanding the varieties of Judaism at the beginning of the Common Era, for it is within this setting that Jesus lived, taught, and acted. Continuity of God's self-giving is reported throughout the canon. The understanding of the acts of God expressed in the Old Testament prepares us for understanding the act of God in Jesus Christ, and visa versa. There is reciprocity between Jesus and this most immediate background; Jesus is understood as reacting both positively and negatively to this setting. Judgment and fulfillment are both operative in Jesus's relation to his religious context.

The Old Testament depicts God's decisive activity in human life, and there are unfolding interpretations of this action.[6] Understanding

---

quintessential Jew, the very Messiah of the Jews" (343). Christians offended by this claim have either denied that Jesus existed (e.g., Arthur Drews) or, more commonly, have held that Jesus or Christ (according to emphasis) was representative of all persons. According to some who hold this view (Adolf von Harnack, Otto Debilius, Rudolf Bultmann, Ernst Käsemann), Jesus's Jewishness was nonessential (343–49). A similar move is made when God is abstracted from the particular Jewish setting and is made "universal" (349–52). The necessary emphasis, according to Osborn, is to recognize the exclusive claim (there is a question whether "exclusive" is the best word here) made by God's explicit choice "realized in the history of his chosen people" (360) and to affirm that Jesus is a part of this tradition. "The truth revealed to Christians in Jesus is that the God of the Jews, the Lord God of Abraham, Isaac, and Jacob, as witnessed in the Old Testament and as incarnate in the Jew Jesus, is the one true God and that this God comes to the world and reveals himself to all peoples only in and through this one people, . . . and through one of them in particular, the Jew of Nazareth called 'Jesus'" (342).

Osborn's argument sets forth the truth in God's specific, chosen people; the relation of Christianity to Judaism; and the embodiment of grace in the historical person Jesus Christ. All this I find most agreeable.

6. Any accurate and generous view of the relation of Judaism and Christianity will want to begin with the conclusion that E. P. Sanders reaches in "Judaism," 372. There, Sanders writes: "Judaism in the time of Jesus and Paul was a noble religion, based

within the thirty-nine texts of the Old Testament is not static. Rather, these texts are an account of the historical dialogue between God and humankind. God consistently takes initiative in establishing the possibility of covenantal relationship. The mode of these initiatives and expectations of covenant participation moves through continually fresh interpretations. Some of these interpretations reaffirm previous understandings; some go beyond, challenging or correcting previous understandings. Examples include the movement to conscious monotheism; the prophetic affirmation of and enlargement of Mosaic covenant themes; and changing interpretations of the nature of God and the nature of faithful covenant life. The Old Testament witnesses refract God's creative and redemptive activity through their own concrete historical situations. Only with knowledge of these developments and their projections into the Common Era can Jesus be responsibly interpreted. That Jesus was a Jew and the sort of Jew he was sets his life into meaningful context.

The reverse relationship is also crucial: the Old Testament is Christianly understood only as it is viewed retrospectively from the vantage point of the proclaimed Jesus of the New Testament. This perspective makes it possible to move through the Old Testament with a sense of relative value in the variety of its accounts. An analogy is the way an autobiography is written from an evaluation of what is most valuable late in life; one rereads earlier experiences, weighing their importance as they are related to the final value(s). Thus, Jesus is both

---

on belief in God's mercy and grace, and inculcating in its members virtuous action and consideration of others. Mercy, in Judaism as in Christianity, begets mercy." The sentiment and the content of the argument are correct. In his more extensive discussion of these matters in *Jesus and Judaism*, Sanders makes several points clear that are of interest in our discussion. Namely, Jesus was not put to death because the Jewish leaders could not tolerate his understanding of or his attempt to embody grace, as Fuchs or Käsemann contend (201); and Jesus did not launch an "attack of grace" against Jewish legalism (274–75, 290). Sanders succinctly concludes: "Thus most of the securely attested facts about Jesus' career also agree closely with what happened afterwards, and what endured from his work is what his message had in common with Jewish restoration eschatology: the expectation that Israel would be restored" (323).

Yet, for all its merit, can Sanders's interpretation explain the Christian movement? Are there no changes in the understanding of grace which are effected by the person of Jesus Christ?

judge and fulfiller of the Old Testament and of his Jewish inheritance and context.

In its origins, Christianity was related to developed Judaism, which was distinctive in its own emergent history in and beyond the Old Testament, to various mystery religions, to varieties of Gnosticism, and to some Greek philosophical movements, such as Stoicism. The reception of the proclamation of Jesus has always been contextually situated. That there is such interaction is a historical given. That these relationships have been creative must also be acknowledged, as must the distractive and distortive effects of these encounters. In any case, the fact that Christianity is influenced and shaped by its religious contexts, as are all religions, is crucial in understanding the character of our response to the New Testament witness to Jesus Christ.

The issue of the relation of Christianity to Judaism must be directly faced. There is a difference in the evaluative response of Judaism to Jesus, and consequently, in Judaism's interpretation of the Old Testament. This difference has made Jews the object of evangelization and rejection, ending in the unspeakable horror of the Holocaust. This history may be responded to only with penance. The Apostle Paul provides a different direction: he insists on God's past and present, pre- and post-Christian purpose for Judaism and the Jews' distinctiveness (Rom 11). The people of Israel continue to have a role in God's providence. In the ongoing interrelatedness of the two traditions, there is much to be learned by each.

In acknowledging Jesus as Lord, Christianity does not set itself above Judaism; there is no moral superiority in either tradition, no preferential status. Rather, there should be recognition of indebtedness and appreciation by Christians of Jews. (Only Jews may speak for Jews; Christians have too often attempted to speak too quickly about and for these members of the family of God.) In acknowledging Jesus as the Lord, Christians must recognize Jesus as Jew. He is a gift of that tradition. But the appreciation is not for that which has had a past purpose and a previous usefulness; it is a continuing sense of God's ongoing gracious intention for all humankind. To acknowledge Jesus as Lord lays upon his followers the moral responsibility and privilege of exhibiting the spirit of Jesus in every relationship.

Grace in Non-Christian Traditions

In our present world, with its access and vulnerability to the panoply of religious sensibilities and practices, it is especially important to recognize this interaction of religious traditions. Perhaps even the emphasis placed upon this fact already reveals an inescapable awareness of this reality. But the character of religious interrelationship must be delineated. Namely, the recognition of grace in other religions, which can and at times does occur through interaction, reveals the extensiveness of grace. As has been consistently emphasized, we are more discovered by grace than we are the discoverers of it. There should be no willful intention to commandeer and utilize for our own purposes other religious traditions. Not to affirm their importance is condescending; to speculate on their soteriological efficacy or failure is presumptuous; to raise their likeness or unlikeness to Christianity is often defensive and offensive; to question their status on a scale of world faiths assumes omniscience. Rather, in encounter we must be prepared to be met with evidence of God's gracious working. Where grace is met, it must be acknowledged, appreciated, and affirmed. Encounter among religious traditions, therefore, is not so much confession but dialogue and mutual witness, that is, sharing accounts of how God is experienced.

Recognition of grace present in other religious traditions assumes that we know in a basic way what grace is. We must know grace to recognize it. For Christians, to say that Jesus Christ is grace is not to say that what is revealed in this One may not be enriched or gain receptive understanding by a range of interactions with other religious traditions. Indeed, it may be legitimately claimed that the value of this engagement is not only that grace is recognized in its multiple expressions, but also that these expressions enrich our appropriation of the meaning of the personal embodiment of grace in Jesus Christ. In this interplay, this hermeneutical circle, we become aware of grace upon grace.

Special note must be taken of the tendency to move the discussion of the interaction among religious traditions to the concern of whether persons outside of Christian faith can be "saved." Soteriological determination is not for human decision. What we do know is the nature of God as expressed in Jesus Christ. This grace is extended to all people and finds expression in God's ubiquitous working. How God judges individual and corporate understanding, faithfulness, unfaithfulness, and willful disregard or rejections, only God knows. What the Christian must proclaim is God's gracious character and its claim for community with God.

The Character of Christian Witness

Acknowledgment of the lordship of Jesus shapes Christian character, but a part of Christian virtue is to acknowledge goodness and value wherever they are found. It is a part of Christian virtue to be clear about differences, to be self-critical and open to judgment. And it is a Christian characteristic to acknowledge the sovereign power of God to dispose through gracious decision. Jesus Christ, who is presented to us, must, in continuity of spirit, be presented by us.

Christianity becomes especially vital where it engages and is engaged by other religious traditions because in such encounter the lordship of Jesus Christ demands to be recognized. The question of the identity of the gospel comes into clearer focus in such interactions. We are reminded that our hope and effort are not for the final triumph of Christendom but of God, who breaks down every wall of separation and who reveals and reinforces every grace through the grace that is expressed in Jesus Christ. In a culturally intermixing world, our daily interchange with all sorts and conditions of people must recognize God's gracious relation to all humankind.

What can we say, Christianly, about those who profess no faith or about those of different faiths? What happens to those who are not Christians? These concerns are held by many Christians. We are often torn between our desire to affirm and acknowledge the value of every person and our conception of the uniqueness and finality of the Christian gospel. Let us remember the faith of the psalmist:

> Where can I escape from thy Spirit?
>   Where can I flee from this presence?
>
> If I climb up to heaven, thou art there;
>   If I make my bed in Sheol, again I find thee.

> If I take my flight to the frontiers of the morning
> or dwell at the limit of the western sea,
>
> even there thy hand will meet me
> and thy right hand will hold me fast. (Psalm 139:7–10, NEB)

As the psalmist declares, the ubiquity, the continuous presence, of God is a fundamental reality. Because this gracious God is unfailingly present with all people, we celebrate the grace of God that undergirds, confronts, and nurtures every life.

God in Jesus Christ did not come to favor a few, to create a privileged minority. God in Christ came with grace free for all, in all, and to all, grace to redeem all humankind. With Charles Wesley we invoke: "Come thou universal saviour, Come and bring the gospel grace."[7]

Christians are sometimes quite un-Christian about those who are not Christians. This is not meant in a sentimental or emotive sense; it is meant strictly: Christians are often un-Christlike—that is, unlike the Christ who comes to every person in radical love and with complete self-giving. We who are Christians must learn to be Christlike toward those who are unlike us in faith.

To claim that Jesus Christ is unique means one has a definitive norm by which truth is judged. It does not mean that there is no truth anywhere else. It is an essential Christian principle that God's presence should be honored wherever it is expressed.

It is possible for us to affirm the value of others at the same time as we affirm the integrity of our own beliefs. It is possible to allow mutual correction and enrichment, even as we hold to the value of our own convictions. We can affirm truth with conviction while we engage in the discussion of truth with an open spirit. In Christian faith, this twofold attitude is possible because it is not our possession of the truth that is significant. Rather, it is our being captured by the One who is truth, our acknowledgment of a Lord who stands over every religious expression, including our own. Christian faith is distinctive not in terms of what it masters, but in terms of that by which it is mastered. The love of truth, not possession of truth, is most basic.

---

7. See the hymn titled "Light of those whose dreary dwelling," in John Wesley, *Collection of Hymns*, 309.

Several years ago a university student said to me, "I don't feel at ease about what God will do to nonbelievers." This unfortunately common attitude implies, "God is gracious and loving, but if you don't believe that, then you will find out what God is really like!" What an indictment of God! Are we more sensitive, more generous, more fair, more merciful than God? We are not—not if God is truly revealed in Jesus Christ. In Christ, God has expressed unique concern, care, forgiveness, and renewal for all people.

From the perspective given in Jesus Christ, we may recognize a "common grace" underlying the created order. In speaking of common grace, we are not attempting to ferret out an underlying natural law, which Cicero described as "the habit of acting as reason and nature demand." From the time of the Greek philosophers until the beginning of modern times, notions of natural law prevailed in both pagan and Christian thought. But we can no longer presume upon natural and rational categories for understanding Christian responsibility. The task of Christian interpretation demands more than the perfection of the foundations and constructs of classical moralists. Rather, we are exploring the continuing and immediate relationship of God to human life in order to determine the character of responsible human life. God's way of relating to the created order is consistent and trustworthy, but it is God's free relating which is of principal concern and of first importance.

God is graciously present with every human soul. There is no place that God is not, and no one with whom God is not. To everyone God has come with forgiving, renewing, sustaining grace. We rejoice in this coming. The generosity of God's grace calls upon us to be generous in our love as we share the forgiveness and renewal of life in Christ.

Grace and judgment are closely linked because there is no cheap grace. Grace is not blind, inexhaustible good will. It is not believing the best in spite of the worse. Grace is God—clearly recognizing the active alienation, the belligerent opposition, and the destructive hate of human beings—engaging, challenging, forgiving, seeking repentance and new being for these hostile creatures. Grace is most clearly known in atonement, in the integrity of the righteous God refusing to overlook or blink at evil, but then taking that evil into the embrace of forgiveness, renewal and hope.

The modes of action are personal. Forgiveness is (to reverse the parts of the word) to give oneself for another in order to reestablish relationship. New life is new relationship. It is to live with another and in that community to find new meaning. Hope is confidence in the faithfulness of the other; it is trust in the steadfast love of another. All of the qualities of life in Christ are initiated, mature, and are sustained through the personal relation that God has established with human beings in Jesus Christ. Atonement is a personal interaction, an interaction made possible by the costly love of Jesus's self-giving.

We inevitably evidence our knowing in our doing because to know the truth is to do the truth. To know Christ is to carry the mind and heart of Christ—even in our fragmented ways—into all the hurting, broken, rejoicing, hoping world. As Charles Wesley's hymn puts it:

> O that the world might see and know
> the riches of his grace!
> The arms of love that compass me
> would all mankind embrace.[8]

Divine grace is comprehensive. Through the life, death and resurrection of Jesus this grace enlivens us and mandates our service.

The grace of God may be discovered in other religious traditions, but grace in human life is not limited to religious traditions. From the vantage point of the grace of God defined by Jesus Christ, we also discover grace in the common life of humankind. In the webs of historical existence, there are intentional acts of self-giving, expressions of selfless generosity and love for others that we can only designate as gracious activity. The ubiquity of the prevenient God implies that every life is continuously engaged by God, and in ordinary living of daily life there are positive responses to God's grace through the mode of human relationships.

It is an expression of Christian character, as truthful and appreciative, to acknowledge goodness wherever it appears. The gospel is not

---

8. See the hymn titled "Jesus, the name high over all," in John Wesley, *Works*, 7:126.

served by refusal to affirm gracious action or to treat it as though it is not truly gracious. Hence, there is no need to designate good will or human self-giving as "splendid vices" or as possessing the form but not the content of goodness.

More important than Christian attitudes, however, is the claim that God is at work in the totality of human life, and that the search for meaning, the search for beauty, truth, and goodness are responses to God's continually engaging grace. The prevenient grace of God is present to all and for all. God's universality ties all of life together. Anticipations of God's clearest expression of grace in Jesus Christ are both accepted and affirmed.

Because of this ubiquitous, gracious presence of God, Christians often share many ethical values with other people of good will and serious moral purpose. In fact, we often find ourselves in solidarity with diverse groups who advocate justice in particular circumstances, and we may share the stigma of exclusion along with those whose ethical actions have placed us at odds with prevailing authorities and powers. From the understanding of God's grace in Jesus Christ, we are enabled to recognize grace in other arenas of human relationship. We affirm as good that which comports positively with that normative expression.

Contemporary understanding of grace focuses on a passion for righteousness. This passion carries a concern for justice and works through personal and systemic modes of relationship. Hence, recognizing grace in other traditions involves recognizing efforts to serve justice and social righteousness. The recognition of grace is not only in personal and bilateral relations between individuals; there is also the recognition of God's activity among the disenfranchised, the marginal, the hungry, and the dispossessed. Relations among religions demand a critical view of the way in which religion itself is understood.

The obverse must also be recognized, namely that relationship offered may not be accepted. Grace, although extended, may be rejected. Hence, the grace defined by Jesus Christ may also reveal the gracelessness of human interaction. In this way, grace may come as judgment, as a clear criticism of the quality of life and of the demeaning of existence. Again, reciprocal interaction is a basic dynamic of authoritative life structuring.

We do not understand grace as a special quality of every life but as a relationship that God, as divine agent, intends with every human being. We are dealing here not with the grace of nature but with the nature of grace, whether embodied in Jesus Christ or in the universal grace that characterizes God's presence in all life. In Jesus Christ is expressed what God everywhere and always is: a person who is actively engaging every person in forgiveness and renewal through self-giving love: "From his fullness have we all received, grace upon grace" (John 1:16, RSV).

The grace of God in Jesus Christ draws to focus that which radiates through God's relationship with every human being. That which is manifest in Jesus Christ represents both an exclusive center, which brings God's activity most sharply to focus, and an inclusive reach, which relates this specific event to all events of God's grace in human history.

Grace in Experience and Theology

Grace is identical with Jesus Christ in person, word, and deed. He is the self-giving of God to humankind.[9] Above all in his death, Jesus set forth the grace of God in a new, inward covenant of grace, extending divine forgiveness, renewal, and restoration to believers. Jesus asks his disciples to show the same God-like initiative in generosity, in the overcoming of evil with good, in the love of the hostile and undeserving, in the conferring of benefits on those who cannot return them, and in unlimited forgiveness.

Thomas Aquinas and his successors looked at the double pattern of grace from every angle and attached various adjectives to the aspects they saw. Their intention was to describe different operations or effects of grace rather than to say there are different kinds of grace. So, for example, where uncreated grace is God (the Holy Spirit), created grace

---

9. In "Grace," in *Vocabulary of the Bible*, F. Baudraz writes: "Later theology thought of *charis* as a divine attribute, but it would be truer to the New Testament to speak of it less abstractly as the divine love in redemptive action .... Here the Greek word *charis* seems to pass from the aspect of disposition or good will which bestows blessing to the action itself and to the actual gift, but in the New Testament neither the action nor the gift is separable from the person of the giver, God in Christ." See 157–60.

is a supernatural habit infused into the soul, In addition to infused grace, Aquinas also speaks of assisting, cooperating, actual, habitual, sanctifying, prevenient, subsequent, and sufficient grace.[10]

Karl Rahner, Peter Fransen, Jean Daujat, and Gregory Baum see grace as synonymous with God's love or personal presence; it is pure gift, God's way of giving himself. Reformers were not able to clear away all the longstanding problems that arose from thinking of grace not as God's generosity in personal action but as a supernatural "something," such as strength, assistance, or influence, which God gives. There is no sound alternative to thinking of grace simply as a gracious personal relationship, to be thought of on the analogy of the influence of a good father or mother upon a child: "Grace is not something God himself gives us; it is the way God gives us himself."[11] Grace, to the degree that it is grace, is personal. God's grace is given to us in person, in Jesus, and personally calls us to the graciousness of personal relations with God and with one another.

---

10. Influence implies interaction. The great divergences in Christian teaching about grace have sprung from the tendency to isolate one from another.

11. [EDITOR'S NOTE: This sentence is of central importance to the author's thought, and may or may not be a citation. If it is a citation, the editors have to date been unable to locate its origin. In any case, it is the sort of sentence the author would himself conceive.]

CHAPTER SIX

Grace, Disgrace, Grace

"and right perfection wrongly disgraced"

(William Shakespeare, Sonnet 66, line 7)

Christian existence, its contours and content, is shaped by the grace of God present. To live in the presence of God is to live in relation to the triune God. It is to participate in the dynamic, responsive self-giving and receiving of God's inner life extended to creation.

Disgrace

Sin is the denial of God present; it is refusal to respond by self-offering to God's presence. Hence, sin is a rejection of Immanuel, a rejection of Jesus Christ and his way, truth, and life. Sin is disgrace, the condition of living by denying grace. Sin is to live rejecting the favor of God.

There is an order of understanding which operates in the awareness of sin. First, the presupposition is grace. Only as we are encountered by God present do we know what grace means and what it means to reject grace. Denial of grace presupposes awareness of grace. Second, sin is effected by the eclipse of grace, by intruding a projection of false ultimacy (which is idolatry) in the place of true ultimacy, or by violation of grace, attacking the vulnerability of God's exposed self-giving, by destruction of love.

Grace is the presupposition of a Christian evaluation of life. To be discovered by God is to discover who one can and ought to be; it is also to discover who one has been and ought not to be, as well as to discover the contrast between the two. Being discovered by God brings knowledge of right relationship (righteousness) and false relationship (unrighteousness).

The dynamic of positive relationship is the work of God present in Jesus Christ as effected by the Holy Spirit. God's initiative is necessary for human self-discovery. But that self- discovery may respond to grace with gratitude or rejection. The rejection of grace is a rejection of God. Sin is God-denial, giving oneself to something other than God, as though a person, object, or ideology were the supreme value.

We repeat a basic theme: knowledge of true relationship makes false relationship recognizable. The description of the dynamics of positive relationship provides the sharp contrast by which negative relationship is known and lived out. No life is relationless. Relationships established create the formation of personal and corporate life.

The qualities of the one to whom or the object to which a person is related determines the quality of the relationship and the quality of life formed by that relationship. Relationship created by God present constitutes the most basic and fulfilling relationship. This relationship establishes the believer in Christ and then leads to maturity within the body of Christ. Relationship with God releases the most complete potentiality for the human self.

Rejection of grace issues in malformation of life. To attempt to live as though God is absent atrophies human possibility. Life is limited by the god one worships. The richness of the dimensionalities of that to which one is related determines the potential richness of human personhood.

Rejection of grace is not only personal and individual; it is also systemic and corporate. Rejection at a systemic level is the organizing of social life in disregard of or in opposition to the presence of God, so that social, political, economic, or personal structures are idolatrously given primacy in value and are acknowledged as dominant or commanding. God present is denied by antitheistic construction of corporate existence through unjust, enslaving, and marginalizing treatment of persons; through racist and sexist social constructs; through economic exploitation; and through violations of peace.

The true depth of human sin is recognized when sin is understood as a violation of God's love, not of God's law. In both personal and social malordering, sin is a positioning of life over against God's proffered presence. Sin is an attempt to escape God by turning to a false god. As denial of God present, sin is the pretense of living in the absence of God.

Although presence may be denied, God is not absent. God's presence is ubiquitous, steadfast, persistent, unfailing. But the divine presence may be disregarded or rejected. Thus, alienation is a human phenomenon: the human denial of God. God's presence is vulnerable, for God comes with invitation, which allows the possibility of rejection. The truest knowledge of sin comes through the clearest awareness of grace. Oddly enough, the closer one is to God, the more acute the awareness of any distance that exists.

Alienation from grace is not primarily a lack of knowledge, an intellectual mistake, or simply cognitive estrangement. Rather, the basic alienation is contrariety of will, a willful turning away, an intentional substitution of value. Sin is the positioning of oneself so as to avoid, escape, or attack the persistent presence of God.

In the light of grace, it is possible to understand what it means to live as though grace were absent. "The more clearly the covenant of God is known to be a *gracious* covenant," Helmut Gollwitzer writes, "as a covenant of forgiveness, the more acute becomes the consciousness of sin."[1] Only when life is set within the horizon of grace does gracelessness take on its true character, and only then is there acute consciousness of sin. A primary implication of this perspective is that it is in terms of the cross—the full expression of God's effort to overcome alienation—that we are able to understand sin. Sinful life is ungracious life lived opposed to grace; it is disgraced living.

The Rejection of Grace

If Jesus Christ is truth, then sin is a lie. Jesus Christ as incarnate truth reveals the truth about God and human beings. Jesus reveals who we are in new community with God and neighbors. Sin rejects this truth; as such, sin is a denial of grace and denial of community with God and neighbors. This denial distorts human existence. Because sin is a lie

---

1. Gollwitzer, *Introduction*, 162. Emphasis in original.

about human life, sinners must deceive themselves about its character and value. Indeed, Scripture calls Satan "the father of lies" (John 8:44). The life of sin is a false and inauthentic existence, which requires self-deceit for its persistent power.

Sin represents response to authority, but to a false and limiting authority. To be a self is to have a god; to be a community is to share a sacred center.[2] But the character of the god one worships, the sacred center a community shares, shapes what the self and community become. Sin produces malformed life because it is idolatrous; in its wake, both personal and corporate life become misshapen. Because sin has to do with relationships, it is never an isolated condition. Inevitably, all connecting relationships are affected. Thus, sin may be expressed between people or in systemic arrangements in society. Miscentered lives foster injustice in society, manipulation of others, institutionalized self-interest and exploitation, economic abuse, and political tyranny. It is a matter of disgrace that human life is bought and sold, that there is race and gender discrimination, and that there is ecological abuse. Worship of false gods results in false ordering of human life. The heinous fruit of sin is produced by the evil roots of misplaced love.

The fundamental falsehood of sinful life is the promulgation of a lie about God, that is, a rejection of grace as though it demeans, distorts, or disregards life. Temptation always begins with a doubt about God's goodness: "Did God say, 'You shall not eat from any tree in the garden'?" (Gen 3:1). In sin, God's mercy is interpreted as a denial of human integrity or as a restriction of human possibility. In sin, God's grace seems to be either regressive authoritarianism or simply unnecessary for significant human life. Faced with the reality of grace, human beings deny grace as they misconstrue God and what relation to God means. Preferring human autonomy or the self-sufficiency of human relationships, sin perpetuates a lie about human life and its possibilities.

The dynamics of grace, as popularly understood, are often looked upon as an intrusive authority or imposed sovereignty and consequently as a denial or at least a retardation of full human maturation. When grace is viewed as external, authoritarian, and repressive, per-

2. See Shils, "Center and Periphery," and "Society."

sons seeking self-sufficiency, willing to assume responsibility for their actions, and desiring strong self-identity may reject grace as counter to their self-interest.

Grace and Faith

What is the appropriate interaction between God present as grace and human development through grace? How does grace operate? John Oman has correctly set the order of grace and faith:

> Grace is grace precisely because, though wholly concerned with moral goodness, it does not at all depend on how moral we are . . . God's gracious relation to us can have no meaning for us without moral sincerity. But, as it is while we are yet sinners, and to deliver us from sin, to make our moral goodness its condition would be to defeat its purpose.[3]

The interaction of grace and faith is an ongoing theological problem. This issue is more acute because we have stressed the strength of grace, an emphasis which might make the theme of sovereignty overwhelming. For the issue to be set most adequately, the tension should be seen as between grace and faith, not grace and freedom. The most precise way of setting the issue is to ask how grace functions in relation to both divine and human integrity. Integrity affirms the centrality of relationship and of those in relationship. Within relationship and as relationship, grace and faith can most adequately be discussed.

The dynamics of relationship move beyond efforts at discrete determination of what part God's grace plays and what part humans contribute. Thorough interrelatedness as embodied in relationship precludes drawing definitive lines between divine and human activity. For relationship, by its nature, overcomes the distancing of subject and object. Relationship draws subjects together in such a manner as to override self-claim and to prevent calculating proportionality of decision or contribution.

For relationship to remain relational and not to become so engulfing that one is lost in the other, or that both are lost in a greater synthesis, there must be integrity of subjects, so that personhood is

---

3. Oman, *Grace and Personality*, 194–95.

not only retained but enhanced in relationship. Relationship possesses its character as the actualization of the meeting of subjects of integrity; it expresses its character as the integrity of each is drawn forth in the event of meeting; it fulfills its character as the integrity of each person in relation is reinforced. In positive, good relationships two contrary things happen: one is drawn out of oneself; one is reinforced in oneself.

There are priorities in divine/human relationship, for initiative is always attributed to God, the originator of relationship. Such initiative is witness to God's freedom as grace. Human participation in relationship is always responsive. No neat demarcation can be drawn between these two dimensions of relationship; they are held in ongoing tension, each subject of integrity being affirmed by the other.

Nonetheless, as God takes the initiative to be present, everything depends upon God. There is no human possibility without grace. But there is a counterpoint: God present invites responsive presence; self-giving evokes responsive self-giving. The interaction of gracious offer and grateful acknowledgment sets the dynamic of Christian existence. This divine/human symbiotic living in, through, and with one another is the ground of Christian worship, service, and community.

Conceptions of the sovereignty of grace are often controlled more by interpretations of sovereignty than by interpretations of grace. Yet it is precisely the reverse move that is critical. Grace sets the understanding of sovereignty. Grace defines who God is and how God works. Hence, God's sovereignty is a sovereignty of grace.

Themes such as foreordination and predestination, omnipotence and omniscience, find appropriate theological meaning as they are interpreted not as independent categories, which would carry a priori and universal meaning, but as dynamics of relationship, as expressions of grace. Because grace and faith are known in and through relationship, relationship must be explored.

First, grace reveals divine integrity in the freedom of its initiating action. The expression of divine integrity meets human beings in such a way as to call forth their response-ability.[4] Grace is a self-giving of God that creates a self-finding for human being. Initiative is with

---

4. A point earlier made by H. Richard Niebuhr in *The Responsible Self*.

grace; faith is grateful acceptance. Through Immanuel, grace makes clear both who God is and who human beings are.

Second, grace maintains and respects integrity. The relationship between grace and faith is a relationship that preserves and reinforces the integrity of those involved in relationship. To be in the grace/faith relationship is to be drawn out of oneself in self-giving to the other and to be reinforced in oneself through affirmation by the other. Integrity is both retained and enhanced through mutual love and endorsement.

Third, grace nurtures and releases integrity for maturity. Because divine grace allows, encourages, and supports human integrity, maturity (i.e., responsibility as a self-in-relation) is possible. Maturity is manifest in the ability to honor another self and thereby to honor one's own self. By its nature and action, grace makes such maturity a possibility for human existence.

Grace, as God's way of being, establishes our way of being. The integrity of divine grace makes possible the integrity of the faithful responder.

Faith is relational response to relationship offered. Faith is the response of the whole person to the wholeness of the person of Jesus Christ. The authority of grace is not an external power that forces acknowledgment; it is not alien or tyrannical; rather, it comes as an inviting claim that seeks reception. Grace as embodied in Jesus Christ comes at a human level. By the mode of his coming, Jesus establishes the integrity of persons. Grace as person creates and sustains persons in relationship. The integrity of each person is found in the affirmation of the integrity of another.

This relationship is not one that simply involves the isolated individual with Jesus. Dimensions of relationship include participation in a community that transmits the primal relationship. The reality of Jesus is a part of history, part of our past. As historical, however, it also possesses a context, a social character. As a social historical fact, Jesus is known only as bound up with and transmitted through his particular historical reality. So grace as God present comes through the complex process of ritual, rite, liturgy, hymnody, devotional formation, and missional responsibility—all of which are shared experiences within a community. Grace also comes through specific social, political, economic, and cultural contexts. The church is a community of grace, so God is present in the worship, service, and life together of a corporate group. God present also makes claims upon the surrounding social environment. Integrity, as a result, is grounded in grace as present in Jesus Christ and is reinforced through gracious community. Human integrity is established and affirmed in covenant.

Personhood is not an originally given fact. We are born human beings; we must be loved, coaxed, and nurtured into being persons. Personhood is found only through progressive realization of the meaning of relationship and community. Life is established by the gracious overture of God and matured in reciprocation, in response.

Three descriptive elements characterize the grace/faith relationship: the creative, preservative, and promissory qualities of relationships. If faith is response, then that which calls faith into being is the determining factor in the quality of faith. God present as grace creates Christian existence, which is then expressed in gracious living. Grace evokes graciousness.

Relationship must not only be created, it must also be preserved. God's steadfastness (*hesed*) invites human faithfulness. Faith is a continual referring of life to God, a continual responsive affirmation of God. Faith creates character, and character is found in integrity. Integrity is faith as continuing faithfulness, as faith being faithful. From God's side, this integrity is the character of grace, however surprising to human unfaithfulness; from the human side, integrity is the reflected character of responsiveness.

Faithfulness to God expresses itself through faithfulness to others. The love of neighbor is a proper response to God present; grace begets grace. Graciousness springs from grace and is expressive of grace. Grace issues in gracious service of others and in shared life with others. Christians must learn to love as love has been expressed in Jesus Christ (John 13:34). There is a qualitative affinity, so that the faithfulness of God elicits enduringness in human relationships.

There is also a promissory, hopeful quality found in relationship with God. Reflective of the constancy of God, responsive self-giving endeavors to reflect constancy. Faith as integrity is the placing of one's future into the keeping of God. God's presence conveys confidence that extends into the future. Because God present is unlimited by time or space, we live in hope and we live by hope. Christian hope is an ineradicable ingredient in God's relating to humankind.

To live as a mature person in our historical context is to live by grace. We are to live not only with thanksgiving but also as those responsible for creative self-giving, enduring faithfulness, and hopeful service; that is, we are to live as those responsible to God and to the neighbor. Such responsibility is expected of those who have been transformed by grace and now live "in Christ."

The power of grace is the persuasion of love. God present creates, preserves, and fulfills relationship. In this divine/human relationship, integrity is both source and result.

Grace, Disgrace . . . and Grace

Gordon Rupp once spoke of "the optimism of grace."[5] A Christian's basis for hope, the optimism of grace moves through the reign of sin in human life, a reign that has marked the natural and social contexts with tragic destructiveness. Grace encounters annulling realities as persistent presence. Where God is present, hope lives. Indeed, to recognize that our world is fraught with self-destructive and other-destructive force is itself a work of grace. Grace both enlightens and enlivens. Both awareness of problematic existence and hope of redemption characterize gracious sensitivity.

Actual transformation is effected by gracious, particular relationship. Grace is not known abstractly but in God's actual self-giving in history; in Jesus Christ and in the Spirit's presence, there is renewal of human life. Hope does not defer to the future; hope reshapes the understanding of the past and determines life in the present. We live transformed in and by hope. Hope remakes actual life. It does not merely project what might come after this present time. The future of hope restructures the present. God's presence brings past, future, and present together in new being.

To be graced is not to be given a possession or to be benefited in a way that other less fortunate persons are not. Grace is a proffered per-

---

5. Rupp, *Principalities and Powers*, 64–78.

sonal relationship that is then also offered through those who respond to God's presence by their presence with others. Those who receive grace are to share grace; indeed, the reception of grace is evidenced by the sharing of grace. These two aspects of receiving and sharing cannot be separated. To sunder reception and giving is to destroy the very nature of both reception and giving. Jesus is the paradigm.

Trinitarian Relationship

The God Christians worship is irreducibly triune. The Christian understanding of God is not monotheism plus Christology. To find life through relationship with God is to participate in the life of the triune God. Worship of God is therefore relational and corporate. In worship, we are made participants in the corporate, interactive life of the Godhead.

In the revelatory event of Jesus Christ, we are found by a giver (First Person), through a giver (Second Person) and through reception by a receiver (Third Person). To "know" God is an engagement of the total human person, affectively and volitionally as well as cognitively. Givenness and reception are brought to sharpest focus in the crucifixion, where God, in profoundest self-giving, identifies through self-separation with that which is alienated from God. But also in profoundest self-giving is a self-giving of God to God. Throughout this relating–disrelating–re-relating is the essential interrelating of the three persons of the Godhead.

That human persons are drawn to live in interrelationship with the triune God is the deepest mystery of Christian existence. Incorporation into Christ means incorporation into both the living reality of Christian community and the living reality of the divine life.

To say that grace is Jesus Christ is to claim that grace is the triune God's way of being. God is in Christ; the Holy Spirit is the Spirit of Christ.[6] As grace, God's steadfast love comes continuously to share life with human beings.

---

6. In his *Treatise on Grace* Jonathan Edwards affirms that grace is God present, but he places the emphasis on the Holy Spirit rather than Jesus Christ. Edwards writes: "*where this holy Divine principle of saving grace wrought in the mind is not merely nor chiefly that it is from the Spirit of God, but that it is of the nature of the Spirit of God*"

Beyond grace, there is disgrace, and beyond disgrace, there is, once again, grace. Beyond alienation, God is reconcilingly present, and distorted human life is drawn into affinity with God's shared existence.

As John Bunyan long ago wrote:

> When the day that he [Mr. Honest] to be gone was come, he addressed himself to go over the river. Now the river at that time overflowed its banks in some places; but Mr. Honest in his lifetime had spoken to one Good conscience to meet him there, the which he also did, and lent him his hand, so helped him over.
>
> The last words of Mr. Honest were, "Grace reigns." So he left the world.[7]

(55, emphasis in original). Again, "Grace in the heart . . . is no other than the Spirit of God itself dwelling and acting in the heart of a saint" (70).

Edwards argues that in the economy of God's relation to human beings, the Holy Spirit, the Third Person of the Trinity, is present: "*Though all the Divine perfections are attributed to each person of the Trinity, yet the Holy Ghost is in a peculiar manner called by the name of Love*" (57, emphasis in original; cf. 67). He insists that "All of the grace and comfort that persons here have, and all of their holiness and happiness hereafter, consists in the love of the Spirit" (66). Edwards, as is evident, agrees with our central assertion that grace is God present. He differs in that he makes the Holy Spirit the normative presence, whereas we have been stressing a christological center. The reason for his emphasis is his understanding that the Holy Spirit is the Trinity expressing itself as love. Our concern has been to identify grace clearly, hence our stress on Christology.

Both emphases work from a Trinitarian beginning point. The entire Trinity is present in each expression of the Trinity. The presence of the Holy Spirit is the presence of the triune God. The difference between Edwards's approach and my own makes clear the interaction of the persons and indicates that Christology must not be thought of in exclusive terms. In order to clarify what grace is and to stress its personal character, we have taken the incarnation as our point of reference.

7. Bunyan, *Pilgrim's Progress*, 323.

Bibliography

Adams, Robert M. *The Virtue of Faith: And Other Essays in Philosophical Theology*. New York: Oxford University Press, 1987.
Allmen, Jean-Jacques von. *Vocabulary of the Bible*. Cambridge: James Clarke, 2002.
Aquinas, Thomas. *The Summa Theologica of St. Thomas Aquinas*. New York: Benziger, 1912–25.
Barrett, C. K. *The Signs of an Apostle: The Cato Lecture*. London: Epworth, 1970.
Barth, Karl. *Church Dogmatics*. Authorized translation by G. T. Thomson et al. Edinburgh: T. & T. Clark, 1949-.
Braaten, Carl, and Robert W. Jenson, eds. *Christian Dogmatics*. 2 vols. Philadelphia: Fortress, 1983.
Bunyan, John. *The Pilgrim's Progress*. Arranged by E. W. Walters. Nashville: Cokesbury, 1939.
Calvin, John. *Commentary on the Book of Psalms*. Translated by James Anderson. 2 vols. Edinburgh: Calvin Translation Society, 1846.
Cobb, John B. Jr. *A Christian Natural Theology: Based on the Thought of Alfred North Whitehead*. Philadelphia: Westminster, 1965.
Daiches, David, *God and the Poets*. The Gifford Lectures 1982–1983. Oxford: Clarendon, 1984.
Davies, W. D. *Paul and Rabbinic Judaism: Some Rabbinic Elements in Pauline Theology*. London: SPCK, 1948.
Dawkins, Richard. *The Blind Watchmaker*. London: Longmans, 1986.
Dunn, James D. G. *Unity and Diversity in the New Testament: An Inquiry in to the Character of Earliest Christianity*. Philadelphia: Westminster, 1977.
Edwards, Jonathan. *Treatise on Grace: And Other Posthumously Published Writings*. Edited with an introduction by Paul Helm. Cambridge: James Clarke, 1971.
Ernst, Cornelius. *The Theology of Grace*. Notre Dame, IN: Fides, 1973.
Flender, Helmut. *St. Luke: Theologian of Redemptive History*. Translated by Reginald H. and Ilse Fuller. Philadelphia: Fortress, [1967].
Gollwitzer, Helmut. *An Introduction to Protestant Theology*. Translated by David Cairns. Philadelphia: Westminster, 1982.
Hanson, Anthony Tyrell. *Grace and Truth: A Study in the Doctrine of the Incarnation*. London: SPCK, 1975.
Hick, John. *God Has Many Names*. Philadelphia: Westminster, 1982.

Hopkins, Gerard Manley. "As Kingfishers Catch Fire." In *The Later Poetic Manuscripts of Gerard Manley Hopkins in Facsimile*, edited by Norman H. MacKenzie, 106–7. New York: Garland, 1991.

———. "God's Grandeur." In *The Later Poetic Manuscripts of Gerard Manley Hopkins in Facsimile*, edited by Norman H. MacKenzie, 96. New York: Garland, 1991.

Jaroff, Leon. "Roaming the Cosmos." *Time*. February 8, 1988, 56–60.

Jennings, Theodore W. "A Tradition of Encounter and Transformation." *Ministry and Mission* 9 (1983) 1–2.

Jeremias, Joachim. *The Central Message of the New Testament*. Philadelphia: Fortress, 1965.

Johnston, Robert K., L. Gregory Jones, and Jonathan R. Wilson, eds. *Grace Upon Grace: Essays in Honor of Thomas A. Langford*. Nashville: Abingdon, 1999.

Jüngel, Eberhard. *Death: The Riddle and the Mystery*. Translated by Iain and Ute Nicol. Philadelphia: Westminster, 1975.

Langford, Thomas A. "Distinctively Methodist: Christian Conference." Address given at the United Methodist Council of Bishops, Lake Junaluska, North Carolina, 1999.

———. "Focus on Faculty." *Duke Divinity School Bulletin*. November, 1963.

———. *In Search of Foundations: English Theology: 1900–1920*. Nashville: Abingdon, 1969.

———. "Notebooks of Prayers." Unpublished.

———. *Practical Divinity: Theology in the Wesleyan Tradition*. Revised edition. Vol. 1. Nashville: Abingdon, 1998.

———. "Religion and Sound Learning." Sermon preached in the Duke University Chapel, December 8, 1985.

Manson, William. "Grace in the New Testament." In *The Doctrine of Grace*, edited by W. T. Whitley, 42–55. New York: Macmillan, 1931.

Moltmann, Jürgen. *Religion, Revolution, and the Future*. New York: Scribner, 1969.

———. *The Crucified God: The Cross of Christ as the Foundation and Criticism of Christian Theology*. New York: Harper and Row, 1974.

Neville, Robert C. *God the Creator: On the Case for the Transcendence and Presence of God*. Chicago: University of Chicago Press, 1968.

Niebuhr, H. Richard. *Radical Monotheism and Western Culture*. New York: Harper, 1943.

———. *The Responsible Self: An Essay in Christian Moral Philosophy*. New York: Harper and Row, 1963.

Oman, John. *Grace and Personality*. New York: Macmillan, 1925.

Osborne, Robert T. "The Christian Blasphemy." *Journal of the American Academy of Religion* 53 (September 1985) 339–63.

Outler, Albert C. "Shaping the Christological Dogma." Address. Emory University, Atlanta, GA, January 1963.

Poteat, Patricia Lewis. *Walker Percy and the Old Modern Age: Reflections on Language, Argument, and the Telling of Stories*. Southern Literary Studies. Baton Rouge: Louisiana State University Press, 1985.

Reumann, John. *Creation and New Creation: The Past, Present, and Future of God's Creative Activity*. Minneapolis: Augsburg, 1975.

Rorty, Richard. *Consequences of Pragmatism*. Minneapolis: University of Minnesota Press, 1982.
Rupp, E. Gordon. *Principalities and Powers: Studies in the Christian Conflict in History*. London: Wyvern, 1965.
Sanders, E. P. *Jesus and Judaism*. Philadelphia: Fortress, 1985.
———. "Judaism and the Grand 'Christian' Abstractions: Love, Mercy, and Grace." *Interpretation* 39 (1985) 357–72.
Schillebeeckx, Edward. *Jesus: An Experiment in Christology*. Translated by Hubert Haskins. New York: Crossroad, 1981.
Shils, Edward. "Center and Periphery." In *Center and Periphery: Essays in Macrosociology* (Chicago: University of Chicago Press, 1975) 3–16.
———. "Society: The Idea and Its Sources." In *Center and Periphery: Essays in Macrosociology* (Chicago: University of Chicago Press, 1975) 17–33.
Silone, Ignatio. *Bread and Wine*. New York: New American Library, 1963.
Stewart, Claude Y. Jr. *Nature in Grace: A Study in the Theology of Nature*. Macon, GA: Mercer University Press, 1983.
Swinburne, Richard. *The Coherence of Theism*. Clarendon Library of Logic and Philosophy. Oxford: Clarendon, 1977.
Tillich, Paul. *Systematic Theology*. Vol. 1. Chicago: University of Chicago Press, 1967.
Torrance, Thomas F. *Divine and Contingent Order*. Oxford: Oxford University Press, 1981.
Toulmin, Stephen Edelston. "The Recovery of Practical Philosophy." *American Scholar* 57 (1988) 337–52.
United Methodist Church. *The United Methodist Hymnal*. Nashville: The United Methodist Publishing House, 1989.
Wesley, John. *A Collection of Psalms and Hymns*. London: Strahan, 1741.
———. *A Collection of Hymns For the Use of the People Called Methodist*. London: Wesleyan Conference Office, 1877.
———. *The Works of John Wesley*. Editor in chief, Frank Baker. 26 vols. New York: Oxford University Press, 1975-; some volumes, Nashville: Abingdon, 1984-.
———. *The Works of John Wesley*. 3rd complete and unabridged edition. 14 vols. Peabody, MA: Hedrickson, 1986.
Williams, Charles. *Descent of the Dove: A Short History of the Holy Spirit in the Church*. Grand Rapids, MI: Eerdmans, 1939.

www.ingramcontent.com/pod-product-compliance
Lightning Source LLC
Chambersburg PA
CBHW030905170426
43193CB00009BA/737